A NOVEL BY
SUSAN EVANS MCCLOUD

BOOKCRAFT
SALT LAKE CITY, UTAH

The characters in this book are fictitious,
and any resemblance to actual persons,
living or dead, is purely coincidental.

Library of Congress Catalog Card Number: 92-85090
ISBN 0-88494-852-8

First Printing, 1992

Printed in the United States of America

This book is for
Heather McCloud-Huff,
who bears the courage, calm, and beauty
of the Scottish women who
were her forebears

Preface

During the period of Scotland's history when this story begins, the Union of 1707 had just joined Scotland and England. Although many profit-minded men could recognize the political and economic advantages to both countries, the majority of Scotland's people considered the step a betrayal and resented the loss of sovereignty and the terms imposed upon them by their more powerful neighbor. Following the victories that William Wallace and Robert the Bruce had won over the English in the early 1300s, Scotland had been an independent, self-ruling nation for nearly four hundred years. The spirits of the people never willingly submitted to English rule.

In the mid-1500s Henry VIII, with a fanatic's passion to dominate in every possible sphere, invaded Scotland. He enticed Scottish noblemen into his service and began the political maneuverings which would culminate with James, the son of Mary Stuart, Queen of Scots, being placed on the English throne. James would rule both countries, becoming James VI of Scotland and James I of England.

At the time this story takes place, English statesmen feared more than anything else a Stuart restoration. In 1715 James Edward, living in exile in France, led an uprising in an attempt to regain the throne. His father, James, had been forced to flee the country, due largely to his Roman Catholic convictions, and the English then offered the throne to his Protestant daughter Mary and her Protestant husband, William of Orange, who became joint sovereigns. Although James Edward's attempt met with failure, Jacobite (a term derived from the Latin name for James) sympathies remained a source of real concern. When "Bonnie Prince Charlie," James Edward's son, arrived in Scotland in 1745 with only a handful of men and a heart full of dreams, many of the chiefs of powerful Highland clans supported him half-heartedly. Though they recognized his weak and unfavorable position, they preferred the risk of the attempt to the continuing influence of England—so bitterly resented—in their lives.

Following the disastrous defeat of Charlie's forces at Culloden Moor, the Scottish people suffered at the hands of the English as never before. The clan system was, in essence, broken; and many of the chiefs who had now become landlords emptied the Highlands of people and repopulated them with sheep. Many powerful Scotsmen, crafty enough to see where advantage lay, "sold out" to the English in exchange for influence and ease.

By the early 1800s the Industrial Revolution was in full swing, and change was becoming a constant and overwhelming influence in people's lives. Robert Burns had revitalized the spirit of his country-men with his stirring verse, and Sir Walter Scott had delighted all of Britain, commanding respect and popularity and establishing the novel as a fresh, significant literary form. Religion was undergoing a great upheaval. Education, always stronger in Scotland than the rest of Britain, was also experiencing reform. In the cities poverty, overcrowd-ing, and the chaotic progress brought by mechanization strained men's abilities to adapt and devise. The climate was favorable, the time ripe for the Mormon missionaries to glean a bountiful harvest in the lands of their forefathers.

Scotland would not again stand as an independent power among the nations, but her power over the feelings and imaginations of her people would weave a heritage of poetry, romance, and loyalty which would endure to bless the lives of thousands of her stalwart sons and daughters, many of them American by birth, who proudly maintain:

> From the lone shieling on the misty island,
> Mountains divide us, and the waste of seas;
> Yet still the blood is strong, the heart is Highland,
> And we in dreams behold the Hebrides.
>
> —Walter Scott

Anne

1707

1

$\mathcal{A}$nnie could feel the sun beating too hot on her head, forcing her eyes to squint against the glare of it. Perhaps the man gazing at her with such a fixed, thoughtful expression would find her unattractive if she squinted hard enough. *But it is too late for that now!* she reminded herself. What was it Dougall Macpherson had said? She had heard the words, but their meaning floated away from her into the empty, silent void which seemed to exist around her. Unaccountably she heard the mew of a curlew overhead and the bawl of Bonnie's new calf from the open byre. His breakfast was late. That was Annie's fault. She should be tending to her duties, not standing here with the sun in her eyes and this tense, tall man bending over her.

"I know it seems sudden to you." Mr. Macpherson spoke as a gentleman, his words measured and proper. She shivered a little beneath the hot sun. "Surely you have expected this, Anne. Known, really, save for the moment of its coming." He exercised deliberate patience, seeming not to mind her awkward silence. "Well, 'tis all settled now, and in a month's time we shall be man and wife, and you the lady of a fine house, my dear."

What more could she ask? He was offering her station and respectability she had never dreamed possible—escape from the harsh, dreary life of a farmer's daughter into the pampered ease of wealth and privilege. Words! Beautiful, airy words that had beguiled her father and mother but that held no enchantment for her.

She shrank inwardly as he reached for her hand and pressed the soft flesh to his lips. "Annie," he murmured, and his voice was to her like the rustle of dry leaves which the autumn wind lifts and rattles.

He seemed to assume that she was already happy in merely contemplating her good fortune, and he appeared oddly undisturbed by her lack of response to him. She watched his shiny black coach bounce and sway along the rough, uneven lane leading from her father's cottage to the main road that wound through the small village of Kingussie up to Macpherson's estate. Then she wiped her sweaty palms along her skirt, walked to the byre, and pulled her work apron from the hook by the door. She was late for the chores, which threw off her entire day's schedule; she would have to work longer than usual and perhaps risk a scolding. And, of course, it would be just that much more difficult for her to slip away after supper in search of Gregor. And escape to Gregor she must. She could make it through the tedious hours of the long day if only she knew that Gregor waited at the end. Beyond that she refused to think. She dare not, for fear something inside her would snap. She lifted the heavy iron bucket and ducked into the first stall, where Bonnie waited, watching her with wide, rather mournful brown eyes.

Merely the sight of him made something inside her go weak with pleasure. She ran the last stretch of field that separated them and threw herself against him, breathless and panting. He held her at arm's distance and lifted her chin with his hand so that her eyes were forced to meet his. The touch of his warm fingers on her skin sent a shiver of delight tingling through her. "Gregor, my love!" She shook free of his hold and covered his mouth with her own. He returned her kiss, but not her hunger and ecstasy. It seemed she could taste his sadness, and she drew back with a gasp. His eyes, the blue as gray and unlighted as a winter sky, held her and calmed her more surely than any harsh words could.

"I know why you've come, Annie. I know what's happened, and that this is good-bye between us."

A cold terror swept through her. "Have ye no help for me, Gregor? No help at all?"

He did not move. His dull eyes betrayed nothing. "'Twould be no help to you to pretend, as we've done before. To hope, when the time for hoping is past."

"Is it, then?"

"You know it is, Annie!" The pain had crept into his voice. "You must make the best of it, and there will be many good things in the life that awaits you. You will come to see that in time."

"And yourself?"

"I will learn how to live without you."

She turned from him, despair tightening the lines of her body. Gregor continued, his voice toneless again. "Your parents have struck a bargain that poor folk like us only dream of; you know that, Annie. They're not about to let go. You must do as you're expected to. There is no way to gainsay it."

"We could run away." She whirled back to face him, her voice trembling, her eyes pleading. But he only shook his head slowly. "No sense in that. We have no money—Macpherson would make short work of us. You would be forced to go back with him, and think of the shame and suffering—"

"Think of me married to him! He's twice my age, Gregor, old enough to be my father. Does it give you no pain to think about that?"

She realized her cruelty too late; her words bit into him like shards of ice. She saw him wince, and his eyes grew as troubled as the sea in a sudden squall.

"I love you, Annie. I will always love you. There's nothing more I can say." As he spoke, Gregor turned away from her. She was never to know for certain what her own response would have been. She felt a thick hand close around her wrist and pull her back sharply, so that she stumbled to keep her footing.

"I'll have none of this, daughter! Gregor MacBain!" Her father's rich voice sang out like a bell and pulsed through the still air like the tight, painful pulsing in her temples. She struggled against his bruising hold on her arm. Gregor turned. His eyes met her father's cold, angry gaze without flinching.

"You leave my lass alone. I'll flog you to within an inch of your life if I ever catch you near her again." He snarled out the words. "She be dead, as far as you're concerned, lad, from this moment on."

Gregor showed no emotion. "I understand, sir." Although his voice shook, his words were firmly spoken. "You'll have no trouble from me." He turned on his heel, not even glancing toward her, sparing her neither a word nor a sign. Her father half dragged her home through the wisps of gray evening. She knew she was crying—more a soft, animal-like moaning, really, that weakened her muscles and shook through her frame. She felt more bruised by the tirade of her father's words than she did by his strong fingers digging into her flesh.

"You be a shameless, ungrateful lass, not worthy of the favor bestowed upon you. Are ye foolish enough to destroy your own life and your family's only hope?" He gave her hand a hard tug. "Wicked daughter. Shameless girl!" His words filled the night, filling her head, crowding out all else, becoming the embodiment of the pain which was the only sensation that stayed with Anne when her father flung her into her room and slid the heavy bar across the door to secure it behind him. She huddled alone on the floor, in the farthest recess of shadow, as though nothing could find her there. But she brought the pain with her; she was the pain, moaning and shivering in the darkness, alone.

While Anne suffered, Gregor grieved in his own way. He stayed out in the woods all night, avoiding human contact. It was his sister, Kate, who found him the next morning. "I thought you would be on the rocks by the stream, or here under the rowan where you first opened your soul to Annie Lockhart." She spoke the words simply, though with an obvious tenderness. He covered his face with his hands. "It is enough," she said, placing her small, warm hand on his shoulder. "Come home with me, Gregor."

He took her hand and allowed her to lead him like a child, though she was six years younger and a mere slip of a thing. He appeared resigned and calm enough, following her in a docile, half-dazed way, his eyes on the ground. "I can't live without her, Kate," he muttered. "I let her believe that I could—so she would go! But I don't truly believe that I can!"

Kate said nothing. She merely held his big hand firmer and kept her steady pace. She and Anne had been best friends since childhood; she, too, would be losing something when Anne went away. *Poor lad,* she thought, listening to her brother muttering under his breath. *Are ye destined, then, to know nothing but pain?* So she wondered as she wound her way, with care and patience, through boggy stretches of peat and rocky recesses toward the cottage where her mother and the little ones waited, in need of Gregor's help. If his heart be broken, still his arms were strong and his back was straight. And there was more work for that back to bend to than he could hope to finish in the daylight hours remaining.

Kate lifted an arm and waved it like a supple young branch to the woman who stood watching them from the door of the low cottage. "We're here, safe and sound," she called. Gregor had stopped his mumbling, and he lifted his eyes, but they were still as dull and sunless as a cloudy morning. And when his mother waved her hand and called out to him, he seemed not to have seen or heard her, and replied nothing at all.

By the time her father unbarred the door the following morning, Anne had made some decisions; she only prayed she might have strength enough to carry them through. At first she had thought to sulk and whine, and complain of her lot, in hopes of sympathy or some miraculous and merciful alteration; now she had no such hopes. She knew Gregor had spoken the truth, harsh as it was; if *he* could not, or would not, help her, there was no help for her here. She would prove quiet and obedient, and let them have their way with her. But she would keep her heart to herself. No one would know what she felt, or even what she was thinking. Her real self belonged to no one at all—not to these people who had coldly betrayed her, and certainly not to the man who had purchased her.

Annie's mother watched her daughter with an obvious relief that turned Anne cold inside. *She cares nothing for me, only for what she sees for herself in the bargain. So be it.*

Anne knew her own judgment was a little harsh and narrow. Her parents, though they lived in a two-room cottage built of stones and clay and thatched with heather, still had the status of tenants. They leased land from the laird and, as was the custom, their tenure in the past had been always uncertain, renewed on a yearly basis, never for any longer period of time. And what progress could a man make that way? Especially since Scotland had suffered seven consecutive years of destructive summer rainstorms that continued into the harvest months. And, following the storms' devastation, winter came early and proved particularly long and severe. People such as themselves lived on the sharp edge of survival; many they knew fared even worse. With Anne's marriage to Dougall Macpherson her father would receive a lifetime lease to the land and a tidy sum—the exact amount still eluded her hearing—which would allow him to reclaim the land, develop new fields, coax a decent living for himself and his family. So, something within her admitted grudgingly, there was just reason for her parents' rejoicing. But what about herself? She would pay the price of their security and happiness for the rest of her life!

The days passed too quickly. She went about her routine, the way she always had, but now there were wedding preparations to tend to as well. From somewhere—Dougall's hand, she was certain—came fine Nottingham laces and watered silks and the creamiest satin she had ever seen. She was to have not only a wedding gown but a wardrobe of dresses to match it: morning dresses, riding dresses, dresses for tea, tartan smocks and blouses, bodices and petticoats— things Anne had never seen. She was accustomed to the plain *arisaid* which fell from her neck to her feet, pleated and belted, and clasped at her breast with a broach. Her only headdress was a linen scarf that hung in tapered folds down her back. Her mother was a fair hand with the needle, so, with help from the milliners and seamstresses the laird sent along, they were able to create the beautiful frocks her mother gazed upon with such envy.

Would they all were hers, Anne thought hotly, *and I running barefoot through the fields in a loose, soft cotton gown, with my love!*

Anne had grown up knowing she and Gregor would one day marry, knowing they belonged to each other. Macpherson had been simply the laird—the man her father paid rents to way off in the big house. She saw him on public occasions; he was nothing to her, in no way a part of her life. Oh, why did he have to take notice of her? Was it possible she had not seen Gregor for weeks, had not even set eyes on him since that dreadful night? She cursed her father at the very memory of it! Kate had been here a few times, but Anne's mother frowned and grew silent in the girl's company, and Kate noticed the reticence and was naturally stung by it. What harm could Katherine do? Pass notes between the anguished lovers? Arrange secret trysts?

I have no life of my own, Anne thought bitterly, gazing at her image in the low, clouded mirror, at the beauty she had taken for granted, that was no more than a fact of life: the perfect nose, not too long, not too pointed; her fair, dewy skin; thick amber hair that curled in wild tendrils of its own accord; deep-set hazel eyes bordered with lashes as dark as her hair; an elegant neck and small, demure, ladylike hands— all the elements to make her marketable, marketable enough to attract even a rich man! A man with titles and wealth, a man willing to pay for her beauty! She felt powerless and frightened, and there was no place to hide, no shoulder she could cry on, no heart to which she could pour out her longings. Everything had been taken or changed.

The days melted away as hoar frost in the spring melts before one's gaze. Anne saw Mr. Macpherson seldom, and then only in the company of others. He was always patient and soft-spoken and appeared to be solicitous of her welfare. But so would a kind uncle be, or a friend of the family's. To marry such a man, for a showing of kindness? To live with him, day and—night! At times the prospect struck terror to her heart. The future appeared as a dark cavern she was fearful of entering. She could find nothing to light her way. Marriage wasn't the end of her road; rather, the beginning. But no one spoke of what her life would be after her wedding day. No advice, no instructions, no training for the duties ahead. What did her own mother or the other women around her know of the duties and cares of a wealthy laird's wife? She stood at the mouth of the cavern alone, unaided, feeling she faced a frail future—a future as uncertain and elusive as a will-o'-the-wisp in the low marshes along the riverbank.

On the morning of her wedding she felt the same stunned half awareness she had felt when Dougall Macpherson had proposed to her. She stood docile while Katherine and her mother dressed her, indifferent to the effect of the startling white goldthreads and starflowers Kate wove in with her curls. She brought only one thing of value with her, one thing that was really her own: the Lockhart ring. She had always known it would be hers when she married. It was so old that no one living remembered its origins; it was said that nearly two hundred years earlier an ancestor, a goldsmith by trade, had fashioned the ring for his bride. It was a most singular piece of jewelry: a vivid, scarlet red ruby cut into the shape of a heart, and the heart lay cradled in the palm of a delicate, curving hand. The Lockhart symbol magnificently interpreted. For did not Simon Lockhart of Lanarkshire accompany Lord James Douglas in the year 1329 on his sacred errand? Did not the two valiant and tender men bear the heart of the great king, Robert the Bruce, to the holy city of Palestine? An honor indeed. Marked for remembrance ever after in the family coat of arms. Marked for her in this one possession which proved that noble blood ran in her veins, too. *Macpherson is not the only one with a history to be respected,* she thought as her mother slipped the band over her slim finger. A thrill shuddered through her at the touch of it, though it seemed a loose fit, in danger of sliding over her knuckle. She straightened it into place.

"Mind you don't lose it, lass," her mother cautioned. "Age will flesh you out some. Guard it well until then."

She turned her hand round and round to admire the precious gem. After this day she would wear a wedding band on her other hand, linking her to a new line—a new past, a new future.

As she went to the kirk she noticed that the hawthorn was in bloom. The air smelled of warmth and green growing things, and the sky above her was as blue as Gregor's eyes. When she entered the parish church where she had been christened as an infant, she gasped in astonishment. The dark gloom of wood and stone had been transformed by flowers, hundreds and hundreds of bright spring blossoms woven into garlands that draped the benches and hung from the windows, bouquets that spilled over the chancel and spread in patterns at her feet; Anne felt as though she were walking through a field of wildflowers.

Her pleasure was caught in her eyes, and when they met Dougall's, merely by chance, she was surprised to see a corresponding joy leap like a light in his own. Her wee sister, Janet, walked before her, scattering rose petals that sifted down to rest without a whisper on the polished wood floor. The beauty assailed her, so that she lifted her head and thought for the first time: *This is my wedding—friends and strangers are watching me and for months after will discuss what happens this day. None shall find cause to criticize the bride's spirit or propriety.*

Thus she proceeded, and found she enjoyed standing before the minister and staring up with wide eyes, aware that all other eyes in the kirk watched only her. Her voice rang out warm and true when she spoke the vow, and if her breath caught in her throat for a moment, she had no time to think of that now. As she turned to retrace her journey down the long aisle she caught a glimpse of her mother. Some of the finery *had* been intended for her. Dougall Macpherson had proven quite generous in seeing that the mother of the bride was also properly and pleasingly attired. *She is really quite pretty still,* Anne thought.

Then she was suddenly swept up in a wave of people pressing toward her: laughter and light voices, ladies touching her gown, and gentlemen kissing her cheek. She felt Dougall tug on her hand and then lift her effortlessly into the carriage. There were flowers everywhere; the smell was intoxicating. She remembered his hand on her arm, warm and firm. Then suddenly his lips closed over her lips, with no warning at all. His kiss was sweet and lingering and stirred a sensation within her that made her gasp and draw back. She had never kissed any other man save Gregor, and she would never kiss Gregor again. This man had a right to kiss her, to caress her. She closed her eyes, not wishing to follow her errant thoughts.

The carriage swayed up the hill. She could hear the singing and laughter of people following after and the sharp call of pipes in the morning air. She turned in her seat and waved at the bright mass of faces. As the carriage slowed and drew up at the broad doors of Macpherson's great house, Dougall lifted her out and kept his warm hands pressed against her waist until she, with a trembling, shy reluctance, lifted her eyes to meet his. She noticed for the first time the narrow, fine line of his nose; the strong, jutting chin; lips that were tight, but not too thin—the lips of a purposeful, powerful man.

"There was never a prettier bride in all of Scotland, Annie." He whispered the words against her hair. She could feel his breath on her cheek. Tingling all over with that lovely sensation, she walked through the door on his arm.

The festivities lasted for days. Annie danced until her feet ached, passed from lad to lad, then back to Dougall, but never to Gregor—never his voice, never his face. And the pipes, always the drone and high trill of the pipes in her ears: *She's wooed and married and a'*, they sang. So much meeting, smiling, curtseying, turning her cheek to be kissed by whiskered and heavy-breathed men. And the feasting! Annie had never seen such eating and drinking. The tables sagged with mutton and venison; geese dressed with their feathers to look as though they perched, still alive, on their plates; cheeses and scones and oatcakes; large platters of salmon and trout; not to mention the sweetmeats and pastries and pies. There was enough food, she was certain, to feed the village folk from now till All Saints Day. To her frugal mind it seemed a terrible waste.

There were quantities of barley whiskey—that which was called *uisge beatha,* the water of life—raised dozens and dozens of times to drink her health and Dougall's, while men chuckled and clapped one another on the back and passed the bottle deasil, or sunwise, as had been done since the beginning of time.

And, in time, the last of the guests stumbled off or seemed to fade into the hazy aftermath. Annie felt dull with too much drink and too much food. When she came down one morning she walked the rooms in sudden dismay. What to do now? The question had never concerned her before. She came out of the dayroom to find Dougall standing there, watching her. He leaned with an almost insolent ease against the heavy frame of the archway. His eyes were too penetrating; they always made her feel ill at ease. The look in them now was similar to what she saw in them by candlelight, at night, when they were making ready for bed. She coughed into her hand to cover the awkwardness.

"They're truly all gone," he said, answering her unspoken question. "We have the entire house to ourselves, and the entire morning." He lifted an eyebrow and his gaze narrowed. "What would you like to do, lass? Take a walk round the gardens, go for a drive?"

She was afraid of being alone with him, but perhaps even more afraid of being alone by herself. "No," she hazarded. "I am tired of idle sitting and strolling in close places. I want to ride. Have you horses we can ride?"

He threw his head back and laughed. She was not used to seeing him like this; he had always been so staid, so old, so proper before the wedding. But he seemed full of surprises since then. "We have horses, lass. Would you prefer a roan or a dapple gray, or perhaps a chestnut mare?" The laughter was still in his eyes as he regarded her.

"In truth," she replied, feeling a little flushed, "I prefer a horse that will be easy to ride."

"We can accommodate that," he said, reaching for her hand.

It took no time at all to cover the ground to the stables. Dougall saddled his own horse while the groom saddled the small white palfrey he had selected for her. It felt strange to ride off beside him. She had been accustomed to working each day. This sort of leisure, following one's own pleasures and fancies, sat uneasily with her.

"Enjoy the time while we have it," Dougall called over his shoulder, as though reading her thoughts. "'Twill end soon enough, lass."

Anne did not wish to enjoy his company. Had she not promised to keep her heart to herself? Riding through patches of yellow gorse and sweet green grasses, watching the river, clear and swift, run alongside their path, she thought of Gregor and felt an aching disloyalty. Where was Gregor right now? Working in the fields most likely, furrowing and planting. He was the oldest of nine children, although five of those lay in the churchyard. But his father had been dead four long years, and Gregor had shouldered the duties of a man far earlier than most lads did. Was he missing her? Was he sick and grieving?

"Anne, watch your way, lass. The pony is stumbling."

She had strayed off the path to an area where the stubble was thick and matted and strewn with sharp rocks. Coloring beneath Dougall's gaze, she guided her horse back to the narrow walkway.

"We're in the heart of Macpherson country here," Dougall said. "For nearly five centuries my people have lived and fought on this land, have wandered these very river paths where we ride." His voice was soft, seeming to caress the words as he spoke them. Anne knew that the Macphersons were an ancient family, going back to Clan Chattan. But this new softness in the man who had appeared so austere and proper disarmed her. "I have stories I'll tell ye some day, lass." His eyes were as dreamy as his voice. He slowed his horse so that she drew up beside him. "You are a fair addition to the Macpherson line, Anne. What fine, good-looking sons you shall bear!"

She dropped her eyes and fumbled with the reins. She was not accustomed to such talk between men and women. She moved ahead of him along the narrow path, and he let her go. The sun was warm on her hair. Larks, building their nests in the tall grasses, rose in arcs of bright color against the sky, spilling forth their irresistible melodies. And Dougall had begun talking again, with warmth and enthusiasm, drawing her attention, even her sympathy, against her will.

2

_____

"Edinburgh!" Annie stared at him, not caring that her mouth stood open in foolish astonishment.

"I have business to attend to. Think ye that I do nothing but wile my days away here?"

"I have no idea what you do with your days, you must know that!" she cried, then put her hand to her mouth in sudden horror at what she had said.

But Dougall looked up from his papers and smiled. "You'll do nicely, yes." He smacked his lips in sudden satisfaction, a gesture, Annie thought uncomfortably, much the same as if he had just purchased a new mare, made a good bargain of it, and was, therefore, quite pleased with himself. She seethed inside as he turned back to his papers and left her standing, awkward and unsure, before his inattention. After a few moments of silence he glanced up again. "That is all, Anne. You may go about your own affairs now."

_Go._ She nearly sputtered the word out, stung by the obvious dismissal, but fighting a sense of panic as well. For what "affairs" did she have to see to? Were there things he expected of her? Was she supposed to know what they were, automatically? She was too proud to ask him, though in another moment she would likely do more than that—she would likely dissolve into tears on the spot. She drew herself up a little, turned slowly around, and left him, glad to pull the heavy door shut behind her, for she had felt his eyes follow her as she walked the interminable length of the room.

That was the only farewell she had. Within an hour he, and those attending him, set off on the high road to the city. Anne watched from her upper window until the stirrings of dust on the road settled, until there was nothing to see but a still, peaceful landscape of carefully patterned gardens stretching down to the river and, beyond the river, cultivated fields, interrupted here and there by open meadow, scattered now with the flowers of spring. Past the meadow a stand of timber marched into blue-gray shadow over a long, distant hill. Annie gazed until her eyes ached, then turned from the window and walked downstairs.

Everything here was size and spaciousness; her father's entire cottage could fit into the ballroom, perhaps even into the dining room. There were trees surrounding the house itself and an old forest behind it from which the house drew its name: Ravenwood. Anne knew the forest had a history which stretched back to the Druids and the worship of the old gods of stone and stream. She also knew bowmen hunted there for fresh meat for the master's table. The drawing room and the morning room, both on the west side of the house, were graced with bright bay windows that looked over this forest and the intervening gardens. The dining room, library, and ladies' sitting room were across the wide hall. These rooms looked to the east, down to the river, deep-cut and snaking along its uneven path. She had not yet been inside half the rooms in the house. Down a long corridor, at the back of the house, was a new kitchen with a laundry room off to the side. She had seen young maids scurrying back there, faces red, arms sagging with bundles of linen and bedclothes from the rooms where the guests had been staying. Ought that to be her domain? Ought she to direct such activities?

As she stood in miserable indecision a servant's bell jangled in a throaty clamor from the row of bells strung above her head. She jumped, smoothed her hair, and glanced quickly about her. No one had seen her. No one knew where she was, nor cared where she was, for that matter. She tugged at the heavy front door and slipped out as soon as the opening was wide enough, escaping into the cool morning air. She could smell the gardens. They seemed almost to murmur to her.

She ran to the side of the house, past the flowering wisteria and the beds of purple violets that stained the black soil. She pushed past the azaleas, not yet in bloom, the sculpted yew and boxwood hedges, to where a tangle of vines and climbing roses, their pale branches barely starting to green, wound themselves into an arbor, half hiding and disguising the small, humped cottage that squatted just beyond their screening. Annie stopped in her tracks. She had not known this was here. "A lovers' hideaway," she breathed, half aloud. She moved forward with the soundless stealth of a cat, bent on discovering more, but the windows were high and the small panes clouded with dust. It looked as though no one had been here for years. How odd, for the cottage sat just at the end of the gardens, which obviously had been tended with meticulous care. What an incongruity! The cottage now appeared to be more a part of the dank, encroaching forest than the well-kept gardens. She tried the door. It was locked tight. She stomped her foot in agitation. There was nothing enchanting nor mysterious to be discovered—what was the matter with her! Large and far-flung as Dougall's holdings were, they were yet commonplace.

She wandered back through the awakening gardens slowly. *What in the world is there for me to do?* With a sudden longing that took her quite by surprise she found herself missing the strong yeasty smell of her father's small byre, Bonnie's warm breath on her hair as she bent over to milk her, the frothing of the sweet liquid as it rose in the pail. Her unused muscles seemed to ache for the strenuous push and pull they were used to. As she approached the house she circled around the wide building, loath to go back inside. A laundry maid whisked past her, carrying a basket heavy with wet clothes to be hung. She was humming a tune under her breath, a tune Annie used to sing as she worked. For a moment she envied the lass, who knew her place and had work at hand. How quickly the hours would pass for the girl! How sad, lost, and empty they stretched for Anne.

For three days Anne wandered aimlessly, or sat long hours huddled in one of the deep, shadowed window alcoves, staring ahead of her, thinking weak, sluggish thoughts, or thinking nothing at all. When meals were ready someone always found her and informed her. She was served at the table alone, with strict observance of all the graces, most of them unknown or awkward to her. No eyebrows were raised, no questions asked; her behavior seemed to be taken at face value, taken and accepted. Was not she the new lady of the house? Were not ladies expected to behave however they might choose? This had been a bachelor's household, run by servants unaccustomed to feminine assistance or instruction. Of course this routine could continue as before, making no demands upon her. Of course there was no need for her here. There was no need for her anywhere.

On the fourth morning following Dougall's departure Annie awoke to rain, rain pouring from the sky, weighting the thin, newly leafed branches of trees until they hung limp, weeping with the excess moisture. The rain drenched the earth until the soil could not hold it; it rose in cloudy puddles to pock the roads that had run to mud and to stretch like a thin, dark veil over the black, even fields. Rain poured from the eaves of the house and ran in rivulets down the dark windows. The servants shivered and went about their business. But the rain defined the extent of Anne's imprisonment even more cruelly than before.

She wandered the big empty rooms, her footsteps echoing in the unnatural stillness. At last, restless still and depressed in spirit, she settled in the library, where a good fire glowed and crackled in the grate. The library contained hundreds, perhaps thousands, of volumes, all carefully organized, all bearing a Macpherson bookplate, as Dougall had once shown her with obvious pride. The walls were dark, the furniture dark and heavy, but the mullioned windows were long and light. Annie dragged a chair up close to the fire and sat with her legs curled under her, stretching out her hands to the warmth. An unbidden image came to her mind of the cottage at home. On such days as this, when her father fed the fire to a roar, the entire room seemed to reflect the glow and warmth. The scene was cozy, with her mother sewing in the corner, Janet playing under the table with one of her ever-present kittens, John and Willie mumbling over their sums (a rainy-day occupation they had no chance of escaping)—the picture was too painful, too clear. She could see herself sitting at the table polishing her mother's silver pieces, few and precious as they were, and her father, less stern than usual, in the corner opposite her mother, shining his big leather boots or reworking and softening the thick harness leather, his stained fingers moving in a steady, rhythmic motion, the rich smells of polish and leather and peat mingling pleasantly in her nostrils.

She opened the book she had pulled from one of the shelves. She was proud of her ability to read, but these books were difficult for her, and right now the letters wavered through the cold tears that clouded her eyes. She blinked back the tears and sat clutching the thick volume to her. *This is not my world,* she thought bitterly. *What am I doing here?* There was no reply, no comfort in the dark drizzle outside nor from the dark loneliness inside her heart that trapped her as surely as the dismal weather and the chill, empty house.

The rain persisted; spring rain in Scotland was nothing to be concerned over. At length it wore itself out, coming to a sad, reluctant, uncertain end, so that on the day Annie rode out the skies seemed to be dripping still, as her mother's sheets dripped when they were first hung over the lines to dry. She had determined to ride home and

surprise her mother with a visit. She could barely keep her own antici-
pation in check as she turned her horse from the road onto the sloped
narrow lane leading up to the cottage where she had been born and in
which she had spent all her years, knowing no other life. She guided
the animal carefully over the uneven ground, slick with stretches of
mud, strewn with sharp, cutting stones. When at last she dismounted
and secured her mare, she found her fingers were trembling and she
fumbled at the latch. Ought she to knock? Of course not! She pushed
the door open and called out, "Mother, mother! It's Annie. I've come
home."

Her mother looked up from the kettle of soup she was stirring.
"You're in time for a wee bite to eat," she said. There was a smile about
her eyes. "You look well, Anne."

"I do?" Anne laughed to cover the surprise in her voice.

She heard a scramble behind her and turned to see the children
jostling to enter. It was dinnertime, then, the big midday meal. Had
she forgotten the pattern already? Anne always picked at the dainty
foods set before her at Ravenwood, but here there was none of that;
rather there were thick slices of warm, heavy bread and bowls of barley soup with bits and snatches of heaven knows what thrown in. Seeing Janet's wide-eyed face she held out her arms, surprised to watch
the child hesitate and take a step backward. In the awkward fumble
Willie stepped on the hem of Anne's skirt and John cried, "You've dirt-
ied her fine dress now, you lout!" Willie, too, scuffled away.

"Don't be silly," Anne protested. "Come, let me look at you all."
But it was difficult to cover the awkwardness—even more so when her
father, stooped and quiet, entered the room. He raised an eyebrow and
looked her over with a long stare. The stew she had been eager to
share stuck in her throat. Conversation round the table wavered,
though she asked all the questions she could think of and the children
answered them willingly enough.

At length Janet, unable to contain her curiosity, asked shyly, "Does
it take an awful lot of work to run a big house like yon laird's?"

"Must not," muttered her father, "seein' she's here midday, all fan-
cied up."

Annie swallowed and slipped her hands onto her lap, aware suddenly of their unreddened smoothness. She felt ashamed, exposed
before all of them. She looked up to see her mother watching her; did
Anne only imagine the pity she saw in her eyes—and the confusion?
Anne was no longer part of this family. It had been a mistake to come

here. She bit her lip, though she wanted to say, "These fancy clothes mean nothing. Let me don my old work apron, Mother, and fill the wash tubs." She noticed with sudden clarity the faded, patched smock and colorless snood her young sister wore. She pushed her chair back, the scraping sound of it along the rough wood like the scraping cut of a knife in her heart.

"I was a bit lonesome for the sight of you," she said, looking at the spot on the wall above her father's head, meeting nobody's eyes. "It's kind of you to let me barge in this way, but I really must hurry back now." Before anyone could stop her she bent and wrapped her arms around Janet. The child responded immediately and clung to her. Anne loved the familiar smell of her sister, and she pressed her face against the girl's sweet hair for a moment. "William, John . . ." She nodded toward the boys. There were tears in her voice; she hoped her father could not hear them. In a few moments more they would spill into her eyes. "Father . . . Mother . . ." It hurt her throat to get the words out.

"Come again, Anne," her mother called after her. Anne stumbled into the yard. She didn't remember tying the knot in the reins this tight! Her trembling fingers tore at it. Her throat ached with the held-back tears.

She was unaware of the punishing, uneven track as she urged the horse along, eager for the safe obscurity of the main road. As she turned onto the solid stretch of packed earth she was about to give the mare her head when someone stepped out into the road from the foot-path that ran beside it. A woman—a young woman.

"Annie! Anne, is that you?" A thin but strong hand grabbed the mare's bridle and steadied her. Annie slid down to her feet.

"Katie!" With a cry of joy she opened her arms to the girl. Kate's face was as glad as her own.

"You look so beautiful, Anne," she breathed, "as corseted and thin-waisted as a lady." She reached her hand out and ran it along the smooth cambric of Anne's full skirt. Then with a slight laugh to cover her embarrassment she added, "Aye, but you have not yet tamed that wild hair of yours, have you? See how it flies in the wind?"

Anne laughed, the pleasure of this meeting already easing the tight misery of the scene back at the house. *I've missed you so much. I've been so wretched and lonely!* The words were on the tip of her tongue. Just as she opened her mouth to say them, she saw Kate's expression alter and darken. The girl cast her eyes to the ground.

"I'm glad of this meeting for more reasons than one, Anne." She looked up with a sad smile. "We are well met, as they say. For I fear I would never have gathered the courage to come to you, come and beseech at Ravenwood House itself."

"Whatever do you mean, Katie?" Anne's voice was gentle, encouraging the girl to go on.

"I'm sore in need of work, Anne, and I thought there might be a position open at the great house—I'd do ana'thing, I'm not fussy, and I'm a good, strong worker, you know that." Her words were running into one another in breathless consternation.

"I know that well, Kate." Anne's own thoughts were tumbling backwards and forwards in terror. *She thinks me mistress of a great house.* Panic rose in her like bile. *How could I let her see things as they really exist at Ravenwood? I would never live down the shame of it.*

Kate was smiling. "You're more like your mother than you see, Anne. I know how it must be. You've taken the place in hand, dismissed half the help, and usurped their duties yourself, just to be certain all's being done correctly. Not a smidge left to do—I'd understand that." Her words, and the brave smile that accompanied them, ended in a sad little silence. Anne shook herself free from her thoughts and reached out for Kate's hand.

"Not so, Katie. I need—I'd be glad of your company, if nothing else." She smiled. How could she explain? How much did she dare say? "Dougall's in Edinburgh right now, and I'm not that certain of what I am free to attempt in his absence. He is to be gone a fortnight." She figured in her mind, quickly. "Wait this week out and come the beginning of next."

"Shall I, Anne? Only if you need me truly."

"Yes, come Kate. I shall count on it." She smiled broadly, hoping her own insecurities did not show too clearly in her face. She mounted the mare and held out her hand to Katie. The question she most wanted to ask stuck in her throat. "Oh, Kate, I am glad for the sight of you," she murmured as she drew her hand away.

A veiled uneasiness dimmed her young friend's eyes, but Anne's lips were silent—she had not the heart nor the courage to ask: *How is Gregor? How is the lad I have always loved? Does he bide as lonely and uncertain as I?*

With a little sigh she started down the road, turning only once to see Kate standing where she had left her, arm lifted to wave a farewell. Anne was no longer in a hurry. She rode in a thoughtful silence through the misty afternoon, unaware of the rain in her hair, unaware of the gray, gathering clouds overhead.

There was a letter waiting for her when she returned; it seemed an omen to Anne. She walked into the library and sat, stiff and straight-backed in a chair, before opening it. Dougall's hand was boldly drawn and easy to read: "Affairs delay me, affairs of great necessity. I fear I must stay in the city, another week, perhaps another fortnight, perhaps longer." She let the paper fall to her lap. *So be it,* she thought, setting her jaw as she had so often seen her mother do. *'Tis clear I cannot wait on Dougall; 'tis clear I must take my life into my own hands.*

It was cold in the library, with the damp settling of dusk. But this was where she desired to work. She rummaged through the drawers of Dougall's desk for paper and blotter, then rang for Rowena, the raven-haired housekeeper who had been here, she remembered Dougall saying, since he was a boy. When Rowena entered, Anne drew herself up and spoke with brisk purpose, though she felt sick and trembly inside.

"Rowena, I should like the account books brought in for me to go over, and I should like a list of all those who are in the employ of my husband."

Rowena blinked. "Employed in the household?"

"Employed in any capacity whatsoever on his estate."

Rowena hesitated, and so did Anne. What if the woman refused her outright? What would she do? "Did my husband leave any instructions for you concerning me?"

The question disarmed the older woman. "No, heavens no, miss," she replied, before thinking to check herself.

"Well, he did leave me with instructions," Annie continued, pushing the truth, but ignoring that. "I was to organize myself and the household while he was gone." It was a crucial moment; Anne sensed that. A haughty, impregnable exterior might do her much harm. Yet, dared she be real—be her true self? "I believe he was curious to see what I might make of things." A smile teased at her own lips and was reflected in a flare of sudden warmth in Rowena's eyes. "And, to tell the truth, I'm as uncertain of the outcome as he must be." Suddenly both women laughed. "I shall need your help," Anne breathed. Rowena nodded, the welcome warmth still in her eyes.

"You need a bite to eat, something to warm your insides after your ride, ma'am. Give me till half past the hour. I shall bring all you request, along with a good, hot meal. Shall I still find you in here?"

Anne nodded. Rowena swept out of the room, and in the sudden stillness Annie heard the ticking of the clock in exaggerated staccato, a sound that beat in time with the hammering pulse of her heart. *I shall be strong and purposeful,* she told herself, clutching the arms of the solid wood chair. *Like my mother, as Kate said, though I have never thought of myself as being like her. But I know how to work, and I'm strong, and I'm willing.*

By the time Rowena reappeared Anne was ready for her, with a list of questions and subjects to be discussed. The two women worked in unison, heads bent over Dougall's desk, unmindful of time. The drizzle in the air became a steady downpour, and the fire in the grate diminished to glowing chunks and embers. The women worked on, in unexpected purpose and harmony.

Kate came as Anne had directed her. Of course, Dougall was yet in the city, so whatever decision Anne made must be hers alone. But she was becoming accustomed to making decisions in her husband's household. The first few had caused her great pangs of anxiety and self-doubt, and she had made obvious errors a time or two, such as when she attempted to dismiss old blind Davey who sat in the stables all day and did nothing more useful than fork hay to the animals and scratch the lazy hounds behind their long ears. How was she to have known that Davey's father and grandfather before him had served Ravenwood and that he, as a young man, had saved the young laird from a fall and was kept on in gratitude and loyalty, despite his age and his blindness? Ignorance was Anne's worst enemy, but there were always ways to mend her blunders. When Katherine arrived, Anne would put her to work first off sewing a new suit of clothing for old Davey. And she made a note of the fact that he favored wings when roast fowl was served, just as Gareth Keith, the factor, favored new cheese and turnip greens in the spring. And the farm manager, Hector Ewen, liked a juicy hunk of deer fat when the hunters had been successful. The little effort it took to please others paid huge dividends, Anne decided, as she set her course.

Meanwhile, she and Rowena concurred on certain procedures and dismissed the forester's nephew, who was a dull, lazy lad and did little to justify having his name on the laird's payroll. They reorganized tasks in the kitchen, dairy, and laundry so that they could let two girls go and hire only Katherine in their place. How relieved, how grateful

Anne was to present a brisk, well-run household to Katie's eyes—an organization she understood and had the control of.

Now, every morning, early, while the dew still adorned the greening fields and budding flowers and the fresh scent of the morning was sweet in their nostrils, Anne and Rowena met and organized the day: tasks to perform, tasks to postpone, food to purchase and prepare, errands to run, services to render. Anne watched with a sharp eye how things were done, and felt a girlish pleasure when one of her suggestions met the obvious approval and respect of the matron who had run a gentleman's household for thirty-odd years. The fact that Anne would lend a hand and didn't mind getting dirty horrified the proper Rowena at first. But she came to see Anne's actions in a gentler light and gave the young mistress what she called "elbow room," wondering with a lively curiosity what the laird's reactions might be when he at last returned home.

Through Rowena, Anne learned that an absence of this length was not common for the master. "Perhaps it is I who frightened him away," she teased, not entirely in jest.

But Rowena frowned uneasily, smoothing the front of her starched, unwrinkled dress with a nervous hand. "'Tis nothing to speak lightly of, ma'am," she chided gently. "I fear your new husband is detained on more serious matters than business." Anne's creased brow and open, questioning eyes brought a sigh from Rowena. "You know naught of such matters, do you, child? 'Tis the king's business which detains Dougall Macpherson in Edinburgh."

Anne had heard her father talk enough to ask, "What king's business, Rowena?"

But the housekeeper shook her head and her face wore a wary expression. "You speak now of questions sharp and prickly as the thistles in yon fields, Anne. Ask your husband about such matters when he rides home."

So it was. And so the days moved forward, busy and progressive. From the start Katie worked herself smoothly into the flow of the household; Anne had known that she would. Kate was a clever girl with a sunny temperament, yet she kept a sharp eye and improved opportunities when they came to her. She had come and gone three days running, and but little conversation had passed between her and Anne. Katherine did not seem eager to speak; perhaps she felt the difference in their situations more keenly than Anne did. When the week's end came she asked, "Will I see you at kirk tomorrow, Anne?"

"I don't think so," Anne responded. "I believe I shall wait until Dougall's return."

Kate only nodded, but something about her seemed to relax, and she gave Anne a spunky curtsy and a bright little smile. "Early Monday morning, then, ma'am."

"Katherine!" Anne reached for her, but the girl danced away. "Don't tease me so," Anne laughingly scolded. But later, thinking about it as she walked in the cool gardens, she wondered at her friend's behavior. "I shall go to meeting," she decided, quite of a sudden. "'Twould please Dougall, my mother, and even the old minister."

The next morning she dressed carefully, taking too much time, and ordered the carriage late, so that she arrived at the kirk along with most of the village folk who walked the short distances there. She went at once to her seat, to the Macpherson family pew, aware of the glances of many as she moved past. Rather than pleasing her, as it had done the day of her wedding, the attention made her blush uncomfortably, and she felt oddly grateful to sink safely against the hard wood of the bench. *It's not their fault,* she thought. *'Tis I who've changed, who've placed myself apart from them.* Yet the alienation carried a sting, and she wished she might slip out now, before the Reverend Mr. Guthrie began sermonizing, and scurry back home. Seriously considering the idea, she turned in her seat and saw her own family troop through the open door, and just behind them Katherine and her mother with the young ones in hand. Then she felt her breath stop, as though a tight band had closed round her chest and cut off her air. Behind the children came Gregor, and on his arm, leaning so close against him that her fair hair touched his cheek, walked Lindsay MacPharlane.

Annie turned back quickly, straightened her skirt about her, and fussed with the gloves in her lap. A terrible heat spread all through her and pulsed at her temples. Lindsay had long had an eye for Gregor; in the past she had tried to tease and tempt him away from Anne. There had been a few times—how well she remembered them!—when Anne had burned with a seething jealousy. Lindsay with her soft blonde curls and her heavily lashed blue eyes—cow eyes, round and simpering! *Does Gregor really want that?*

The trembling inside her was a terrible thing to control. Sitting at the front of the kirk, as she did, she had no way of watching the pair, but she was tormented all through the long, sonorous, maddening sermon by her awareness of them—by the conjured images that her imagination tortured into hundreds of terrible possibilities.

When the long sermon was ended, the psalming and singing done, Anne rose slowly, aware of the sharp ache in the small of her back. Her legs were cramped from the extended, tense spell of sitting. Her agonized desires pulled her in two opposing directions: she could push her way through the crowd and feed her hungry eyes with the sight of him, despite the pain it would bring, or she could hang back, let him go on ahead, mindful that his deep, canny gaze might discover what she was unable to hide.

In the end she did neither, but moved forward slowly, taking her place in the press of bodies, lost in a kind of daze. When she walked out into the pale, overcast morning Gregor was nowhere in sight. Her carriage stood waiting; Gareth Keith, Dougall's factor, was a competent man. He must have handed her into her seat, for she felt the carriage lurch under her and sway into motion. She sank against the soft cushion and slashed at the tears on her cheeks with an angry hand. *I will not weep for him!* she told herself stubbornly. *He weeps not for me. Foolish woman, to be so tender, so easy to wound!* she thought. But the tears kept coming, and she felt again the weight of the new, strange life which had been thrust upon her. Loneliness clung to her like a damp, chill cloud through the long Sabbath hours, and all her childish hopes seemed futile—wasted on a future she could no longer hope for with relish or faith.

Katherine knew what was coming and stood, prepared to be quiet and docile before the angry onslaught; Anne could see that much in her face. But Anne had decided on a different course of action—she would play nobody's fool in this, certainly not Gregor's. So, firming her jaw, she greeted Kate as gaily as ever and set her about her tasks with an equanimity that took a terrible effort. Katherine was taken aback and bothered so by guilt and curiosity that, after less than an hour, she left her work and came searching for Anne.

"Forgive me, Anne, please. 'Twas a terrible dilemma to know whether to tell you and hurt you, or say nothing at all."

Anne couldn't pretend ignorance of the subject to which Katie alluded. She smiled a weak smile. She would not reveal what she was really feeling—especially to Katie, who was duty-bound to report back to Gregor.

"What your brother does now is his own business, isn't it? I have no hold on his life. If he must take a wife, then . . ." She hesitated. This was not easy.

"Then why Lindsay MacPharlane, that simpering, insincere little vixen!"

Anne blinked, dumbfounded by Katie's vehemence.

"I never liked her any more than you did, Anne, and now to think of her, strutting and proud, having Gregor all to herself." Kate's expression twisted in pain and her little chin trembled. "It wasn't supposed to be like this at all! That's why I need work. If Gregor has a wife to support as well as Mother and the bairns—oh, Annie, why couldn't things have been the way we always planned them to be?" Her words ended in a choked sob, and she threw herself into Anne's open and comforting arms.

"Hush, dearie, don't cry," Anne whispered against her sweet hair. "We must brave it somehow, for what other choice have we?" Her words sounded small and thin above the girl's noisy weeping.

"I don't believe he loves her one whit!" The words were a whispered hiss against Anne's wet sleeve, but they froze in her heart.

"Don't say that, Kate!" Anne's retort was sharp. "'Tis wicked, 'tis useless."

Kate lifted her tear-streaked face. "But 'tis the truth, Anne, I know it. Gregor moves like a man in a daze. He goes through the motions of living; he doesn't care about things anymore."

Anne shook her head as though to dislodge the words that spread like a bitter poison into her brain.

"He told me he didn't know if he could bear to let you go, Anne. And when he did, it was as though something inside him died."

Anne clapped her hands over her ears. "Hush! Hush!" Her voice had grown throaty and pleading. Kate sniveled and wiped at her swollen eyes. Gently Anne pushed the distressed girl away from her. "You go back to your work and put this out of your mind, lass, and I'll do the same."

Kate opened her mouth to protest, but Anne shook her head and turned such a gaze upon her that Kate scurried off to do as she was bade.

When Kate was safely gone Anne sunk into a chair and covered her face with her hands. It was not difficult to picture Gregor standing before her, his hair tousled by the wind, his eyes sparkling and warm, as warm as the touch of his lips over hers. She could smell hay and molasses on his clothes and feel his rough coat rub her cheek as she nestled her head against his broad chest. She could hear his voice, husky with emotion—

"Anne?"

Anne jumped at the sound of her name and grasped the arms of the chair.

"Is something the matter?"

"No, Rowena, I just felt a bit faint for a moment, that's all." She rose with as much spirit as she could and brushed past the woman who stood watching her. "I'll check on Maureen and Bonnie in the kitchen to see that they're making the cheeses properly." No one could make cheeses like Anne's mother, and she had taught her daughter well. "Then I believe I'll spend an hour or two in the gardens."

She didn't look back to see if Rowena still watched her. How much had her wise old eyes seen? Anne drew in deep breaths as she walked back to the kitchens. She must appear normal and in control of herself here. What Kate had said must be put away in some little corner of her mind now, while there was work to be done. She would draw it out later, in the dark, quiet privacy of her room, if she dared— if she found strength enough to bear the agony of it.

She pushed through the broad scullery door and bent over the bowl Bonnie was stirring, struggling to bend all her thoughts and attentions to the task at hand.

3

By the time Dougall returned, Anne had forgotten what he looked like, at least all the little details, those things which distinguished him from "the laird" and attributed human qualities to him. She came into the library one morning for her daily meeting with Rowena and he was there. He rose from his chair behind the desk as she entered, and the warmth in his eyes as he turned them upon her was not unpleasant.

"I'm not a ghost, lass." He grinned as she stood staring back at him. "I arrived far too late in the night to awaken you." He looked down and with a patronizing air patted Annie's ledger and the papers stacked neatly on his desk. "What's been going on here?" He looked up, curious and interested. "Come, Anne, you look as though you take *me* for the usurper!" He laughed, not unkindly. "What have you been up to in my absence?" He patted the papers again.

"I have been running your estate for you in your absence, my lord." She tried to speak the words demurely, but they didn't come out sounding that way.

"Taking your rightful place as lady of the house, I see. Well, very good."

She could not read his expression, but his words sounded straightforward and sincere enough.

"I've missed the sight of you, Annie," he said without warning, holding his arms out. "Come, lass, give me a kiss."

She walked toward him, and he laughed as he reached for her and pulled her alarmingly close. She liked the touch of him; she could feel her heartbeat quicken as his lips covered hers. He smelled of the outdoor air, fresh and clean. When he put her aside with a sigh she felt flustered and vulnerable, but he did not notice; he had already turned back to his desk.

"I've important business to attend to this morning," he said, "but sometime today you and I must confer. Will you meet me here at one for tea?" His head was bent, his face turned away from her. *Yes, my lord; yes, husband; yes, Dougall. Just what should she say? If I can make time for you, sir, in my busy schedule.* That would be more to her liking.

"Am I in your way here?"

She jumped, startled from her thoughts, and looked into his puzzled brown eyes. They were nice eyes, filled with a serene intelligence. Anne backed slowly away. "No, I'm . . . you're fine there . . . I'll see you at tea, then." She choked the words out, but he had bent to his work again and didn't seem aware of her struggle.

I have longed for his return! she marveled in frustration as she stomped down the hall. *But he's right. I don't want him in my library. He makes me feel like a child and takes over as though I no longer existed.*

She found Rowena in the pantry, and they held their meeting in the light, airy sitting room. Anne hid her distress from the old servant, who was naturally glad of her master's return. There was a gloom on Anne's spirit, though the day was sunny and friendly. After taking tea alone in the garden when Dougall failed to appear, she felt a bit dizzy and ill, and rested for an hour in her darkened bedroom. As she drifted off into a light, gentle sleep it was Gregor MacBain she dreamed of, it was Gregor's lips touching hers, and it was his firm, callused hand that led her through the gardens while he spoke sweet, gentle things to her there.

"What's this? What's this, Anne?"

Anne glanced up and sighed. It had been thus ever since Dougall's return. As soon as he discovered or was made aware of a change she had made he would confront her, with a wary wonder that would have amused her if she had not been so unsure in his presence.

"What is it this time?" She kept a mild and pleasant expression.

"Two pair of trousers and three shirts for old Davey, lass?" He scratched at his forehead.

"'Tis not extravagant, as you judge," she explained, "but wise in the long run. Two shirts full-sleeved and coarse for rough weather; one lighter with a sleeve at the elbow. I can launder them this way, you see, and he won't always be filthy as a pig and ruining the material beyond redemption by gross overuse." She wrinkled her nose distastefully, and when Dougall remained silent she went a bit further. "How you can abide bringing gentlemen friends into your stables to select a horse of their liking with him hulking there, like some stinking, rotting shape that appears more ghost than human . . ."

Dougall nodded slowly. "Yes, I can see wisdom in that."

Anne grew bold. "Sir, it is impossible for me to function without the use of your library. I should like—"

"Well, of course! Help yourself. Or can we fit up another room to your satisfaction, perhaps that little morning room behind the music parlor?"

She placed her hand on his arm. "Please, I prefer the library."

He squinted his eyes and stared hard at her a moment; she could never read his expressions! "Fine. But I shall have a smaller ladies' desk brought in for you—my mother's, I think. I'll have Gareth see to it."

"Thank you," she breathed meekly.

"No trouble, my dear." He brushed his fingers over her hand as he lifted it, then suddenly grasped it and pulled her closer. "These few days I've been home have proven a nightmare, Anne, and I don't seek my bed until outrageous hours." He sighed and looked down at his fine polished boots. "I should like very much to visit you of a night, Anne."

Anne lowered her eyes and rubbed the toe of her shoe along the thick Turkish carpet, and gently tugged her hand from his grasp. "I have been unwell of late," she murmured. And her protest was true. She, who had never been the least bit squeamish, turned faint and sick-stomached not only at the sights in the barnyards and fowl pens but at an overly unpleasant odor—even at a strong fragrance of perfume.

"I am sorry to hear that." Dougall's voice was smooth and appraising—unruffled, as it had been back in the days when he courted her. "Well, we shall see."

She left the room with the faint impression that she had amused him. That night he did come to her, and she was surprised at the pleasure his caresses and tenderness brought. But the next morning, as though to prove herself an honest woman, she threw up the small breakfast she had eaten, nor could she hold down her afternoon tea. And walking in the gardens, even though she sought the cool, shady patches, sent her knees trembling and made her feel light in the head.

She said nothing to Dougall, but set her jaw and tried to ignore it, and the following day she felt better again.

The week's end came and Dougall insisted they attend meeting; 'twas only seemly after the laird's long absence. Though Anne shrank inside, she walked up the path, her arm linked with her husband's, her eyes straight ahead, her head tilted at as high and proud an angle as she dared. The service seemed long; the small of her back ached, and her temples throbbed. She had not seen Gregor enter and had to guess at his presence, at the possibility that he may be seated in a position where he could be watching her.

As they left the kirk Dougall turned to speak to a gentleman, and Anne moved on her way. It had rained during meeting. She lifted her full skirts and carefully picked her way over the muddy puddles that had settled in the low chipped flagstones. She must have tripped over a tuft of grass pushing through one of the cracks; it could have been nothing else. She felt herself lose balance and sway precariously, then firm hands on her arms steadied her and pulled her forward and out of the path.

She knew who it was before she looked up. She paled as her eyes met Gregor's, as she drank in the deep blue shine of them. His hands still held her, and he was terribly close. She attempted a smile, but knew that her face merely twisted awkwardly.

"Oh, Annie," he murmured, "you look like an angel. Are you—is everything well?"

Her chin trembled as she started to speak, so she only nodded her head. Then Gregor's hands dropped from her arms, and she heard Dougall's voice from behind her. "Thank you for assisting my wife, sir." There was no affront in his tone, but he reached for her gloved hand and turned her abruptly, wrapping his long arm round her shoulder. She hazarded one last glimpse of Gregor and noticed that Kate stood at his side. If Lindsay was with him, Anne had not seen her.

Anne was quiet during the ride home, and Dougall did not press her; he sat in a thoughtful silence of his own. No questions were asked about the incident in the kirkyard, until the following morning when it was approached in a roundabout way.

The morning was well organized, the girls busy about their tasks. Anne herself was in the laundry, overseeing the pressing of Dougall's shirts, when one of his men appeared and informed her that her husband had need of her at once; she would find him in his gun room. When she entered, the mingled smells of leather, powder, and oil made her head reel. She steadied herself with her hand on the back of Dougall's old overstuffed chair.

When Dougall turned to greet her his face was dark. "You did not tell me that you hired Katherine MacBain to work in my household." His voice had never sounded so belligerent. Anne shrank inwardly but attempted a brave face.

"I let go two girls who were slovenly at their work and hired but one who is most cooperative and efficient."

"But Katie MacBain—I saw her here with my own eyes this morning!" He shook his head in anger at her demure composure. His mane of hair, still thick and dark, loosened and fell in tendrils over his forehead. "I'm not a fool, Anne. Gregor's sister has no place here. You must realize that."

"I realize nothing of the kind." Anne's heart was racing, and her words wished to tumble forward with the same urgency; with painful effort she slowed them. "She is my friend; it is coincidence only that she is his sister as well."

"Ye have other friends, surely." Dougall's voice was a growl.

"I have not—not like Kate. We've been as sisters since childhood. Dougall"—she paused—"I have no contact with my family. My whole world has changed. I'm lonely for things that are part of myself. Katie does no harm here. I swear it."

Dougall looked up. Anne was surprised at the dull dejection she saw in his eyes. "I do not want her here. You may do as you choose, but remember, it is not my desire that she be here."

This time he left her, brushing past with no further word. She sank into the chair, feeling weak and shaken. He would not have his way! Trying to bully and shame her into complying with his will, with his unkind, unreasonable desire. Kate stayed. And, of course, Dougall took note of it, and his attitude toward Anne remained cautious and aloof. Sunday's rain persisted; the days were dark and drizzly, the nights damp and chill. Near the end of the week the clouds rolled over the low hills, and a clear, warm sun lit the well-washed landscape, dried and softened by a cool breeze the rain had left behind. Dougall could not resist it. "We're going riding this morning," he told Anne. "The weather is perfect for it."

She did not oppose him. The idea appealed to her, too. They rode along the river, and he showed her his fields ripening with turnips, which he used for winter fodder for his own stock and sold at a good profit to others whose undernourished cattle needed fattening in order to bring good auction prices. He owned more land than she had suspected. Beyond the turnips stretched oats, golden white in the bright sun, and one long field of green crawling beans. Dougall seemed at ease and let the horses choose their own pace as he surveyed the beauty and order around him.

"To possess all this! To know it was of your doing, and your keeping . . ." Anne sighed as she spoke the words.

Dougall stared at her thoughtfully. "'Tis yours as well as mine, Anne."

"Doesn't seem so. I can't fit my mind round it," she admitted plainly.

Dougall threw his head back and laughed. "You are a wonder, lass, a constant wonder." She saw that somehow she had pleased him, but she sensed no condescension or insult in his open laughter. "With your stubbornness and your penchant for ordering all about you, Anne, 'twill soon be more yours than mine, and I shall stand in the background taking orders from the likes of a small thing like you!"

She laughed in return. She couldn't help herself, really. His good nature and confidence seemed contagious, and the breath of the moving air was so gentle and sweet. They stopped in the shade of a grove of ash trees to eat their meal. Anne was lulled into carelessness and ate with a relish; the fresh air had given her an appetite she hadn't felt for weeks. Then suddenly, leaning back against the cool rough bark of one of the trees, she knew she was going to be sick.

She looked up helplessly at Dougall, then stumbled to her feet and raced to the reedy edge of the river, as far away from him as she could get before having to drop to her knees, shivering with the spasms that shook her body. Of course, he was beside her before she could draw her handkerchief from her pocket. He pulled his own out and wiped her pale lips, then drew her off to a grassy spot and gently helped her down to the ground beside him, draping his arms round her so that she lay stretched out with his chest for a pillow and the temperate breeze on her face. Save for nights, when they were alone in the dark together, Anne had never been this close to Dougall Macpherson. She liked the solid, comforting feel of him, the sense of him. Why did he seem less old to her now? Less tedious and dull?

"What is it?" Dougall asked, smoothing her forehead. "Do you feel better now?"

"I know what it is," Anne sighed. "I just haven't wished to believe it." She turned her head so that he could not see her face. "I am with child."

He let out a sound which sent a strange thrill through her; then he turned her to face him, his pleasure rough and demanding. "Anne, could this really be true?"

"'Tis true, sir. I fear there is no doubt left to the matter."

He threw his great head back and laughed. He seemed so alive, so unrestrained when he did that. "You've made me a happy man, lass. 'Tis what I have longed for, but hardly dared hope for—and this soon!"

"Yes, this soon." Anne sank back, feeling weak again. But she gave him a slow, timid smile.

Dougall bent over her. "Forgive me. For you, young as you are, and this soon after marriage, there must be fears and mixed feelings. But I'll take good care of you, child." He smoothed back her hair and stroked her face with his lean, gentle fingers. "Wait and see. This will make you happy, my darling, I know."

He bent closer and kissed her. But she scarcely noticed his touch, for the feel of his words, like a caress, swept through her. *"My darling," he said! Does he really care for me? Could he possibly love me?*

The thought possessed her as she rode in a sweet lull, cushioned against Dougall on his mount, while he led her pony along. The afternoon was quiet. The breeze blew into a steady, cool wind. Dougall took his coat off and draped it around her, but she pushed it aside. "I love the wind," she said. "It sets off something wonderful and wild in my heart and my head."

She lifted her face to the rough caress of the wind, for the moment not caring what Dougall might think. He said nothing, but she felt his lips touch the back of her head, and his hand rested lightly over hers as their tall, sturdy mount picked his way home.

4

---

*T*hings were different after that morning. There was almost a gaiety in the house. If Dougall still scowled when he happened to encounter young Katie, well, that couldn't be helped. For the following three Sundays Anne talked him out of going to meeting, due to her delicate state. Though mornings were terrible, she could grit her teeth and get through them, and usually by midday the worst was over. Evenings were the best time of all. She spent her evenings in the library reading or sewing, even dozing off if she pleased. Often Dougall joined her. At first that was terrible for her. She felt stiff, ill at ease in his presence. But, my, how the gentleman could talk! He had such a store of knowledge upon such a variety of subjects, and he drew from it with a relish which could not be resisted.

Anne began asking questions. When she saw that he answered them eagerly, pleased by her curiosity, with no sign of pretense, she asked more and more. The learning excited her. As with all the best things in life, the more learning she tasted, the more she desired. And Dougall never tired of sharing his knowledge with her. He would drag down musty old books from high shelves hidden in shadow and read snatches here and there, and at times long passages. In the beginning it hurt Anne's head to concentrate on the difficult, complicated sentences that contained so many words which she did not know. But Dougall always embellished what he read, so that at length the meaning came to her, and with it a quickening, a glow, as though she could feel understanding, like physical nourishment, course through her.

Summer was in her glory. Anne spent hours in the gardens, at times dogging old Caldwell, the gardener, so closely that he would turn and snap at her, and she would retreat for a while. On a tenant farm, vegetables and staples were planted. If a woman held a weakness for flowers she bordered her cottage with them—that is, if she could manage to take time from the endless tasks which consumed her. The flowers of the woods and those along the river were the only ones Annie had known: wild roses, bell heather, corn cockle, and yarrow. But here in the Macpherson gardens there were dozens of cultivated rose bushes of every color and shade, their perfume delicate or heady, but always sweet and alluring to Anne. She like to snip them and bring them into the rooms, bunches and bunches, along with white daisies, tall red poppies, and yellow iris, until the great rooms smelled as lovely as the out-of-doors.

From her mother Anne had learned some herb lore. The poignant, sometimes musty, clinging fragrance of herbs that stayed on one's fingers, she loved. She was consuming gallons of chamomile, rosemary, and mint teas to calm and mildly sedate her and ward off the nausea. In the cool mornings, if she felt well enough, she gathered bergamot, dill, and bay leaves for fresh salads, mint to mix in with the summer vegetables, and rosemary flowers to candy for a treat, which she sent by way of Katie to her brothers and sisters. The angelica leaves and stalks she gathered to cook with the first tart fruits that ripened, and there must always be fennel on hand to cook with fish. She saw to it that a jar of fresh bergamot leaves were sprinkled into her husband's bath water to ease his tired muscles, and she tucked generous portions of fennel among the straw bedding to sweeten it, especially in the stables where blind Davey and the stable boys, Gavin and Simon, slept.

Anne felt her confidence growing. *She* was mistress of this household, and would soon bear her husband a child. She twisted the ring with the blood red heart round her finger reassuringly. Lockharts could manage any challenge, whatever the difficulties, and come out victor, she reminded herself. The crops ripened, the bees hummed in the rosemary, the winding river ran placid and deep. Anne had never known that life could be so gentle and sweet.

Lulled and content as she was, there were still things Anne wanted done. The heather-thatched cottage at the far reach of the gardens was a bit of an eyesore, and, besides, it still drew her interest. She asked Dougall about it one evening, when there was a break in their reading.

"Open the heather cottage?" He looked up, startled, brusque. "Whatever for?"

"Why, to clean and care for it. 'Tis a shambles now, Dougall. Besides, I've a mind to use it—"

"Use it! How?"

"I'm not certain yet. To merely dry my fragrant herbs and flowers, perhaps. It intrigues me, that's all."

"Out of the question." He spoke the words slowly, looking straight at her.

"Why ever not?" Anne leaned a bit forward. "I see no reason—"

"What *you* may or may not see makes no difference here. The cottage remains locked and closed, Anne. Do you understand that?"

She huddled back in her chair, almost pouting. "Of course I don't understand your lack of reason, Dougall."

"Well, you must simply accept it, then." His voice was still tight and unyielding. He eyed her closely. "Anne . . ."

She glanced up at him through lowered lashes.

"Gareth has his orders. If you attempt to cross me in this, there will be trouble, my dear."

"Really, Dougall, you're being cross for no reason and spoiling our pleasant night." She lifted herself out of the deep, cozy chair with what grace she could. "I've tried hard to please you, and this seems such a little request to make." She was sounding childish, and she didn't want that. But he seemed not to notice. His face had hardened into lines of anger.

"Nonsense, Anne. I give you free rein here, and you take advantage of it. Don't tell me anything else."

He is no green boy to be manipulated by a woman's sighs, Anne thought. *I should have known that.*

"When I ask you to respect a decision of mine, I think you ought to comply."

She nodded her head, knowing her eyes were shaded and distant. Then she turned and walked out of the room and went early to bed. But she tossed and turned, unable to relax into sleep the way she did following the long, tranquil evenings with Dougall that she was growing accustomed to.

Near the beginning of the next week Dougall called Anne into the library—called her from her gardens in the middle of the day. Since the night when Anne left in a huff they had not spent one evening together. She avoided his rooms, suffering from the self-imposed restriction yet reticent to give in for fear of losing something—she wasn't quite certain what.

"I'm sorry I've been gone so much of late, Anne." He spoke the words gently, and she noticed that his face looked tired and drawn. "I've missed our evenings together."

She colored in frustrated agitation. Had he been riding out at night, then? On what kind of business? *I've ignored him so thoroughly that I've lost track of his doings,* she chided herself. *How selfish and foolish I am!*

"I called you here because I fear I must leave again. I must leave soon, and when I return I will often be away at night, as I have been." His voice, like his face, was tired and thin. "I believe we should ride to your parents' home before I leave, to tell them our news."

Our news, he had said.

"And I should like to attend a session at the kirk with you, if you think you can bear it. I know the hour is early—"

"Yes." Anne took a step forward. Some voice inside her said: *I can do that for you.* She was feeling suddenly guilty, and remorse did not sit easily with her. Part of her wished to blame this man for her every discomfort; but something else, stronger, would not allow her the luxury.

"We shall do both, if you like, Dougall."

"If *I* like? Are you not anxious to see your kin, lass?" That look of mild puzzlement, with which he often regarded her, entered his eyes. How could she explain her fears, her mixed, inconsistent feelings?

"Of course I am. Tomorrow morning? I can manage that."

"As early as possible," he added, "before it grows warm."

They drove in the carriage for comfort, as only a gentleman would do when honest men were already sweating and working. Anne thought her reception even less open and kind than before. Her family hung back a little in Dougall's presence—all but her father, who became unnaturally loud to mask his discomfort. Her mother's pale eyes lit with pleasure when Anne told her of the child, but she said nothing to show that pleasure. Stiff pleasantries, that was all. And Janet looking on with wide eyes. Too soon it was time to leave.

Anne felt depressed, let down, somehow, as they bounced over the road back to Ravenwood. The loneliness, which had not plagued her for weeks, teased at the back of her mind, like the beginnings of a nasty toothache. Sunday proved no better at all.

The service was difficult to sit through. Dougall's obvious pride in the expected arrival of a child and heir embarrassed Annie, especially when she looked up from a tedious conversation Dougall and his friends were holding around her, to meet Gregor's gaze fixed upon her.

He did not lower his eyes when Lindsay came up beside him and locked her arm through his. Anne thought she would suffocate from the pain that leapt through her like a flame, fanned into life again by the deep, terrible burning in Gregor's eyes.

When Dougall at last took her arm and led her out to the carriage, they were obliged to walk directly past Anne's old sweetheart. She knew Dougall would not stop for any form of greeting, so she, too, hurried by, lacking the strength to face those eyes at such close quarters. They rode home in silence, and after they arrived Anne took to her bed where she tossed and turned, feeling miserable and trapped, feeling lost and light-headed, not knowing what she wanted and not content with one fragment of her life as it was.

Dougall's days were busy; Anne saw little of him. The flowers bloomed with as much brightness and color as before, and the air was as sweet, but the benediction, the mood of peace in the household had disappeared. And although her physical condition improved daily and the nausea lessened, Anne felt worse than before. Thursday night when Dougall did not arrive to share the evening meal with her, she ate in sullen resentment—ate and ate, indulging in a large helping of Bessie's rich pudding dessert. In the night she was sick, and then could not get back to sleep. As the restlessness grew she wrapped her robe about her and padded downstairs; a cup of chamomile tea might help. She sat in the still kitchen, scrubbed clean, as Bessie always left it, and wrapped her cold hands around the hot cup, waiting for the liquid to cool. Dougall would ride off time after time and she would be left here, and then what? She had organized the household; it ran smoothly with a minimum of help from her. She had her gardens and her books, but she needed something beyond that. *Someone* beyond that!

She touched the growing swell of her stomach with a tentative hand. This child would become larger and larger, and she grow larger with it. And when it was born? She couldn't picture it, make it seem real. She trembled as a terrible, wicked thought entered her mind of its own accord: *This should be Gregor's baby. I always believed I would bear Gregor's children, and we would live together, work beside each other day after day—*

She closed her eyes tight to shut out the taunting image, and gulped down her tea, although it burned in her throat.

She had left the book she was reading in the library. Perhaps she should take it with her to bed. It was a difficult one, and the effort required to read it might tire her sufficiently.

Approaching the room, she noticed that the door was partly open and a dim light shone out into the hall. She moved with quiet caution. The clock had just chimed two. Surely Dougall would not be up at this hour! But there he was at his desk. She could see him, back arched at what looked like a painful angle as he hunched over stacks of books, open ledgers, and papers. He was scribbling something; she could hear the scratch of his quill, like a sharp-toed mouse in the wainscoting. He swore under his breath and she caught the word *Covenanters*. She knew where his political loyalties lay, but only generally. She knew he supported the Stuart kings, despite the danger inherent in such loyalty. She had learned he was one of those passionate men who decried the union which had just been effected between his country and England. She knew he was involved. But in what exactly? And for what principles and purposes?

She paused outside the open door. She had best move quietly on. It would be terrible to disturb him, to explain her presence here at this hour.

Dougall lifted his head. He turned and looked at her, as though he had expected to see her. "Annie, come, come inside. Warm your little feet at this cozy fire."

She entered, timid and uncertain, and took her usual chair. He moved his chair close beside her. "Have you been ill, my dear?" He took her thin white hand between his and rubbed it gently. "What a mess things are, Annie! I've neglected you, as well as all else that is dear to me. And for what?"

He spoke through his teeth, as though the mere effort of getting the words out was painful. His face looked weary and drawn, the line of his bold chin even more firmly etched, his eyes sunken with dark shadows beneath them. Without thinking, she stretched out her free hand and brushed it gently across his temples, then pushed back his hair and pressed the cool surface of her palm on his forehead.

"You need some sleep. You work too hard and worry too deeply. What is it that troubles you now?" The words came from her easily, low and soothing. Dougall closed his eyes and allowed a deep sigh to escape him.

"The games men play with each other, lass. Cunning, cold, and deceitful they are."

She kept her hand on his forehead, but rose and moved to stand behind him. He leaned back against her soft body, and her fingers played through his hair.

"Tell me, Dougall. Let me be part of it, part of something that matters."

He sat still beneath her touch. She held her breath. "This much, Annie," he began, "this much I'll tell ye. Change is in the air, and I mean to be part of it."

"Must there be change?"

"If we Scots are to hold our heads up."

"Must we hold our heads up?"

His great laugh boomed forth. "You are the only person I know who can make me laugh, Annie." He drew her hand from his forehead and kissed her fingers. "It's more than that, lass. If we are to *survive*. We're saddled with England's huge debt, and it's breaking our backs, Anne. Did you know our own national debt is less than two hundred thousand pounds and England's is over thirty million?"

She drew her breath in sharply, and he continued. "The tax on salt is crippling our fisheries, and now the queen threatens a malt tax. The majority of our people drink home-brewed ale, not tea and coffee as the Sassenachs do." He smiled, and with her fingers she could feel it in the lines of his face. "Save for fine ladies like yourself who drink their own homegrown herbs."

"And would James Edward be any better? Would he change all that?" Her innocence voiced the question, but he did not laugh. He pulled her round to face him, and she settled down on the rug, like a small cat curled at his knee.

"Whatever failings he may possess, we need a king of our own. We've lost sovereignty, and with that we've lost all! We're a scorned minority—our representation at Westminster will always keep us as such." He was exercised, despite his fatigue and discouragement.

"Tell me more," Anne urged. And although her eyes burned and her stomach ached and her curled limbs grew numb, she listened. Knowledge possessed a strange, restorative power for her—a power that would have been almost mystical if it had not been so clear, so pure. When at last she rose stiffly, with the help of his hand, the sky was growing light in the east. He clucked his tongue, embarrassed at his excess. "Look what I've done to you now!"

She squeezed the fingers that held hers, not knowing what other answer to give. "There is danger in what you do," she whispered as they ascended the stairs.

"Anything worth doing carries some risk with it," he responded. Anne thought about that. And, as if he could discern her thoughts, he placed his hand over her tender stomach. "Think of the risk, lass, right here."

He came into her room with her; it seemed only natural. She curled up in his arms and slept with his chest for a pillow—in an aura of peace she slept, in a net of safekeeping and love—until the noisy birds woke her and the sun streaming through her windows would not be ignored.

5

Annie saw little of her husband during the weeks that followed. He was gone often, riding long distances to meetings at other estates where the men would secrete themselves sometimes for days. Most of the time she could force gloom away from her by a stringent routine, which always included some study, difficult as that might prove. She missed Dougall, and she didn't like that. She fought the insecurity and restrictions of developing a true affection for or dependence on him. Usually what little time they spent with one another was pleasant. But he was often preoccupied, and always tired. At times his face, though lean and handsome still, looked lined and weathered with the years that had marked it, and she remembered how she had felt in the beginning, how she had looked upon him as something disgusting, something only to be spurned.

One day, as she was reflecting upon such things, she noticed that Katherine hung about her near the end of the day, even walked back into the gardens with her. Anne sensed something at once. Kate usually left in a hurry, facing, as she did, a long walk home and then supper to help with and chores to do. Besides, the girl looked down and scuffled her feet along the flagstones as she walked beside Anne.

"What is it, Kate?" Annie asked. "Tell me quickly, for kindness' sake."

Kate still didn't look up. "The marriage banns have been posted. Gregor and Lindsay will marry in a month's time."

"Go on," Anne said hollowly.

"Oh, Annie, why must I go on? Why must *I* tell you this? They will live with her parents because her father is partly crippled and there are no other children at home. Their holding is close enough to ours. Gregor will work both farms, give us all the help that he's able."

"And who'll pick up the slack? Does he expect you to, Katie?" Anne cringed at the sound of her voice, but continued relentlessly.

"She should come to your family, children or no children. That's the order of things. There's no man at all at your place. Gregor will wear himself out working for everyone else, never his own man."

"I know that." Kate sniffled, then took out her hanky and blew her nose.

"There's nothing for it, there's nothing for it," Anne muttered. Before marrying Dougall she had never questioned the order of things. But now, at times, she could not bear the great gulf that existed between Dougall, the landowner, and the hundreds of plain, honest tenants who worked *his* land and had so little to look forward to or hope for, despite their hard labors. And Gregor was one of them!

"Thank you for telling me, Kate." She hugged the distressed girl and walked her to the edge of the big road. Then, feeling wilted by the sun and tired, she went on inside. *I want a husband,* she thought bitterly, *a man who's with me, who is made up of the things I'm made up of. Dougall and I live in the same house, but we live separate lives. I'm always lonely, I'm always alone.*

Lying in her bed that night, not knowing where Dougall was lying or when she might next see him, she tossed and turned. She could not bear the thought of Lindsay MacPharlane possessing her Gregor. A pain deeper than jealousy surged through her when she thought of them as husband and wife, the way she and Dougall were. She closed her eyes against it, but that made no difference. *Never, never will Gregor hold me as Dougall holds me,* she wept. *Never will we two be one.* She shuddered at the wickedness inside her which spawned such weak desires as these she now entertained. Drenched in loneliness and self-pity, she felt like a girl again, not a woman and wife. Would she always be weak and stupid? Right now she didn't care. She wept in her great, lonely bed, in the silent moonlight, where no eyes could see.

She was not weak on the day of Gregor's wedding. She had made it through her own wedding—how far off that seemed now!—she would make it through his. She would die of suppressed grief before anyone marked sorrow in her eyes or despair in her carriage or pain in the tilt of her head.

Dougall was not at home—would he have allowed her to go if he was? Nevertheless, her family rode with her in Dougall's carriage, in grand style. And although she was but three months away from the birth of her child, the dress she had made for the occasion fell in soft folds from the line of her bust and hid her heavy, round appearance. Her arms and wrists were still thin and lovely, so she made sure they showed to advantage, as well as her slender neck. Her hair, as thick and heavy as ever, shone like polished chestnuts, and the curls framed and softened her face. She knew she looked beautiful; she could see it in people's eyes when they glanced at her. She had that glow of expectant motherhood; her fair skin was unmarked and clear. Lindsay was a pretty bride, but far from the most beautiful the village had seen.

The day was cold, the October sun weak and wan that morning. Anne shivered beneath her shawl. How interminable the service seemed! Had her own wedding been like this? It had felt swift and breathless to her—and so charged with magic. There was no magic here, just a common country wedding. Something tugged at her heart—the old longings for the easy and known way. How handsome Gregor was! Glowing with youth and health. He was eighteen years old, Dougall thirty-seven. Was that possible? Anne looked away from Gregor and over the heads and half-turned faces before her.

Each face mirrors, and masks, an inner person, she thought. She looked more closely; almost every face here she knew, had known since before she could talk, since she had been aware of the world around her. *We're all strangers, though, after all,* she thought, wearily. *Does one person ever really know another?* She glanced at her mother, trying to see her through the eyes of a stranger. She looked much like most of the women here. Her face was tanned and wrinkled from exposure to all kinds of weather, yet her eyes were still young. Her eyes were the prettiest thing about her, though too often they also showed dull. *Do I know her?* Anne wondered, *Any better than she knows me?*

Music shattered her reverie. She looked up to see the wedding couple moving with as much grace as dancers toward her. Lindsay's face was shining; Anne saw Gregor reach for Lindsay's hand. For a moment Anne closed her eyes tight. When she opened them again they were gone, they were past her.

Well. So. It was done. Gregor was no longer a part of her life; he and she had gone separate ways. *Is he happy?* her heart cried. *It doesn't matter,* another voice inside her said. *Happiness is not why we are here.*

What is my path? she wondered, as she smiled at her neighbors. *Why am I here?* Haunted by these questions that had no answers, she moved forward into the crowd.

After the wedding there was a restlessness inside Anne. She felt a desperate need to fill her hours and kept herself busy with even trivial, mundane things. She asked questions and poked her nose in everywhere, and since the laird was so much gone, entirely undependable, his men began turning to her. Again she was making decisions she felt were a little beyond her; but the challenge, even the uncertainty, was intoxicating. If she didn't know something, she asked. She kept her eyes and ears open, and the men, liking her unpretentious manner, soon felt at ease with her. If she could learn something she needed to know by reading, she would disappear behind Dougall's tall books, heedless of time or the regular doings of life, so that Rowena learned to look for her and send her safely off to bed before turning in herself for the night.

Hector Ewen, Dougall's farm manager, was plowing the fields under for the fallow winter season. When he asked her if he ought to sprinkle lime in the soil, she returned the question and asked him what he thought. He thought it a good idea and loaned her James Donaldson's book *Husbandry Anatomised* to read. When she had completed it, taking notes and marking pages, she read Lord Belhaven's *The Countryman's Diary*. This was stuff of the future she had her hands on—she felt it! Drainage and the use of fertilizers. Dougall's lands, lying so close to the boggy river, could use that. Enriching the soil with lime was a new idea, but Hector believed in it, and after reading the books, Anne did, too.

She asked Hector if he might rotate plantings differently, resting certain fields between crops. They had turnips—had that been his idea? What about potatoes as well, even though most Scottish farmers resisted them? Hector grinned; with their two heads together they planned great things. Only winter stopped them, blowing in from the highlands with sharp, ragged teeth and gray, ragged skies. Dougall's tenants, too, could profit from what Anne was learning. With a sigh she told herself, *Spring. Wait until spring. Your child will be born, you'll be strong and fit again. There will be new life, new plantings, new ways.*

The cutting winds brought snow earlier than usual. The sky fluttered like a ragged black cape above them, with hundreds and hundreds of ravens, the ravens of the old wood. Their shrill, lonely cries stirred a deep, lonely longing in Anne. She saw to it that roaring fires were built in the library, as she spent more and more time indoors. She had learned from John Caldwell how to put her flowers to bed for the winter, and she and Hector had completed this task. The work for their hands was diminishing now. Fruits and herbs were dried and preserved in the pantry, the meat had been cured, and the hard apples of the orchard were stored. Anne expected Dougall, and expected Dougall. She began to grow restless again.

One night while sitting late in the library, as was her custom, Anne heard a knock at the door. Not a loud disturbance, just a firm, persistent rat-a-tat. She went to answer the door herself. The wind tugged at the visitor's coat, so he held it close with one gloved hand. His face was in shadow, but she knew him before he spoke.

"May I come in, Anne?"

She moved back and he slid silently past her. She pushed the door closed behind him "Come with me to the library," she said, seeing his wild, weary face. He followed without a word. In the lighted room, with the cozy, crackling fire, he no longer appeared a spectre to her. But, oh, he looked bonnie! She wanted to reach out and touch him.

"What thing has brought you here, Gregor?"

He paused for a few breathless seconds. "I've come to warn you, Anne."

Some hand took up a hammer in her heart and began a tight, steady beating.

"The queen's men are after the Jacobite leaders. There have been too many meetings of late—boasting of their three R's, boasting that their king will come to power, if not by act of parliament, then by invasion before August next."

Anne knew what the three R's were: Resignation, Restauration, and Rescission. But she didn't realize that plans were afoot to bring the Stuart king James Edward back from exile in France.

"They discovered the whereabouts of tonight's meeting and planned to surprise them, but the men were warned, and hopefully most made good their escape . . ." His words trailed off and he looked down at the floor.

"My husband. Dougall was at that meeting, wasn't he?"

Gregor nodded, with such genuine sympathy in his face that it brought tears to her eyes.

"I can't tell you his fate, Anne, but I know they will send men here looking for him. You must be prepared."

"Prepared—how?"

"Have the lights out. Be in bed, or pretend to be. Act startled upon their appearance and affronted, but be polite. 'Twould be unwise to offend them."

"The Jacobite cause, Gregor, are you—do you support it?" He and she had never talked of such things.

"If truth be known I think there are very few in Scotland who don't, Annie." Her name, clothed with his voice, sounded like music.

"Even some of the Tory leaders are in touch with James, though they affirm their loyalty to Queen Anne."

"Do you think Dougall will try to come home?"

"No. This is the least safe place for him right now. These men must have arrangements; he'll be canny enough to be safe, Anne."

"So. He has been secretive in order to protect me." She spoke her thoughts out loud, scarcely mindful that she was doing so.

Gregor moved a step closer. "For your sake I hope all will turn out well," he said in a low, soothing voice.

"For my sake!" She repeated the words, but her voice was sharp as a knife. "Nothing is ever done for my sake, Gregor. Do you not know that?"

He lowered his head, much like a chastised child might. She turned, with impatience, away. "You had best go now. Do you think it safe for you to leave by the front entrance?"

"I came that way because it was close to the lighted window, and I know not the house. It is later now, and I would prefer another exit."

She led him round to the kitchen wing where a low, concealed door led nearly to the forest, black in the darkness now. She stepped aside and he began to move past her, but then he stopped. "Anne, I've no right to say aught to you, but I must know if you are happy at all."

"As *you* are happy now?" A demon glared through her eyes at him. But his only swam with a greater tenderness. Therefore, when he spoke she was surprised by the cold emotion in his voice.

"I've no right to speak so to you, but I shall say it this one last time, Anne. I love you!"

She trembled, and swayed against the wall for support.

"I shall never be happy as you and I would have been happy, but I will not waste my life, Anne!" He struck his fist against the hard, unyielding wall. "I will not! And it will grieve me sorely if you waste yours, Anne. I want nothing more than I want happiness for you." He leaned close and kissed the top of her head.

"Godspeed!" she whispered, but she doubted that he heard her. He had already turned and walked into the night and been swallowed by the dark, shapeless expanse as though he had never existed. She stood by the open door a long time before she noiselessly closed it and walked back through the cold, empty house.

Anne did as Gregor had told her. But she could not sleep, so, still wearing a gown beneath her robe, she sat by her long gray window, twisting the Lockhart ring round and round her finger, for courage. The waiting grew so long that at length she fell into a tense, cold half-sleep, and the demand, when it came, startled her all the more. She thought the stout door would splinter before she could clear the stairs and reach it. She drew a deep breath and set her chin before pulling it open. She had forgotten to appear confused and bleary-eyed. But her state of advanced pregnancy gave the men some pause.

"Is your husband at home, ma'am?" the man in the front asked. Anne took him for the captain; she didn't recognize rank. This man looked young to her, not much older than she was.

"What business might you have with my husband at such an hour?" She kept her voice from sounding waspish and realized that, instead, it sounded much like a mother scolding an untoward son.

"We have reason to believe—"

"Queen's business, lass," an older man interrupted, pushing forward. "We must demand that you allow us to search the house and grounds for him."

She was about to acquiesce, succumb to the inevitable, when the idiocy of it struck her. "I will do no such thing!"

"We must insist," said the older man again, with a dark scowl. Anne folded her arms in a tight line. The wind tore at the hem of her robe, and cold air poured into the house. "I've never heard of anything so ridiculous. Think of it for a moment, gentlemen. If my husband is in trouble by the queen's reckoning, or someone else's reckoning—" She noticed that two or three of the men smiled, despite themselves.

But the older officer blustered, "In trouble by fact of his own bold-faced treason!"

Anne clucked her tongue at him, dismissing his dark words with a toss of her head. "Be that as it may, think the matter through, gentlemen. He would be a fool to come home and wait for your inevitable and punctual visit. And if he did, 'twould only be because he had a hiding place so secure he was certain no searching could discover it.

So you and I would shiver and yawn and wear ourselves out through the long night for no purpose at all."

They stood blinking at her for a moment. "'Tis our orders," the young officer said apologetically.

"Well, take yourselves back and report that you were denied entrance by a wife, young and foolish, and in a delicate state, who did not wish a troop of strange men tramping round her house at all hours!"

She began to push the door shut in their faces, still holding her breath, still expecting someone to force it. The older man took a step forward.

"If there is any accounting to be done," she said, "tell them to come to me and I will stand behind my own actions. Good night, gentlemen."

The door closed. Amazed that no one stopped her, she pushed the heavy bolt into place and stood, so still that her muscles ached, listening: the shuffle of boots, the murmur of muffled voices, the scuffle of horses being mounted. The sounds grew distant and dim. Then there was nothing at all.

The silence that followed was unnerving. In the silence she began to tremble at her impudent boldness. She heard the hall clock strike half past two. Stiff and aching she walked back up the stairs and tried to get warm under the bed covers, but she couldn't stop shivering, and her body tensed every few moments, listening for some telltale sound.

At last, exhausted, sleep began to numb her, to draw away all sensation. Why did that small pattering sound annoy her, break through the soft grayness? She lifted her head, propped it on an elbow, and listened. The sound was not loud enough to be coming from soldiers, but it was more than the wind she heard.

She slipped out of bed and approached her window, barely lifting the fold of a curtain. She saw a man's profile below, close against the shadowed wall of the house. The faint pattering came again, stones hitting the brick wall, not quite reaching her window.

She didn't take time to think; she knew she had to go down. Wrapping her robe around her as she went, she walked through the dark library to the windows and tapped against one with her ring. Almost at once the tap was returned. She slid back the latch and pulled the window open a crack. "There's a door round the side of the house, all the way to the end," she whispered, then hurried back herself, refusing to think, acting only on instinct.

She had not really expected to see Dougall when she opened the door, but what she saw brought her hand to her mouth, and nearly the remains of last night's supper as well. The middle-aged man who stood before her was filthy, his shirt soaked with blood, his left arm lacerated, as though a wild beast had had his way with him.

Anne stretched out a trembling hand and pulled him inside. Though his eyes were glazed with fatigue and pain, he spoke at once and to the point. "I am a friend of your husband, nameless to you, if you please, lass. I was pursued and shot at, and I need refuge till first light, and food."

"And help for that wound," she added, glancing quickly at the torn arm.

The stranger drew a ragged breath. "I would not have come if my need had not been sore." His gentle manner and the pain in his eyes broke Anne's heart. She clasped her hands. "What can I do? I dare not put you here, for if but one servant saw you—"

"All would be hazarded," he finished in agreement. "Have you room in a byre or stable?"

"Grooms and stable boys sleep there, on guard. I dare not risk anyone seeing you." She closed her eyes in order to think more clearly, and at once the image appeared. Dared she? She knew where Gareth's keys hung, and most were marked. Even if it were unmarked, she could surmise which was the key to the cottage. It was too well-suited a sanctuary for her mind to ignore.

Decided, she coaxed the man into the kitchen and found bread and cheese and fresh milk for him without the assistance of light, though she had to feel her way with great care. Igniting a long straw in the kitchen embers, she hazarded one small candle to light her way to the servants' quarters. Gareth's keys were right where they should be. She slid them silently off the hook and tucked them into her pocket. Back in the kitchen she found the wounded man leaning against the cupboard with his eyes shut. She shook him gently awake.

Leaving the warm security of the house behind, Anne led the man through the long gardens, weirdly mottled with moonlight and shadow. A noisy wind scuttled dead bracken and bits of dried leaves against their feet as they walked. It was bitter cold. But the moaning wind did not frighten Anne. When they came to the cottage she paused. The man sank to the ground, and she let him rest there while she approached the door, feeling for the lock with her fingers. Back in the house, before snuffing out the candle, she had selected three unmarked keys to try. She drew them out now and tried the first. It did not begin to go in. She tried the second. It slid in and turned, but then solidly stuck. Her fingers ached with the cold. She wanted to cry in frustration. But the last key went in and turned all the way, with a terrible creak and shudder. Anne twisted the latch and walked in.

Moonlight streamed through the windows. As Anne's eyes adjusted she could make out shapes in the shadows: a chair, a small table, a harpsichord—of all things to find here! And was that a couch in the corner?

Her strange guest stumbled across the threshold. With one hand on his good arm and the other in the small of his back, Anne steered him toward the couch. With an awful moan he sank into the softness and lay there, so still and motionless that Anne let out a small cry.

"I am still alive, my dear." His voice sounded wonderfully human and reassuring.

"I shall return with food and blankets, and something to bandage your arm," she whispered. "I'll lock the door behind me. You are safe here."

She scurried back through the wind and shadows. Once in the house, among familiar things, her hands worked mechanically, without the usual corresponding functioning of her mind. She placed the food in a waxed cheese bag with a drawstring round it and brought clean rags, a bucket of water and, from her herb shelf, a handful of comfrey to sprinkle over the wound to stanch the bleeding and start the healing process.

Weighted down, dragging the awkward water bucket, Anne found the trip back to be tedious and hard. How many minutes or hours she spent huddled over the suffering man she knew not, but when she left him at last he was peacefully sleeping, the lines of pain smoothed from his face. She had reminded him of how close the forest stood behind them. She hoped he would remember when he awakened. With a reluctance she could not understand, she turned and crept out of the cottage.

The sky was beginning to lighten in the east with a few streaks of pink, pale, unlit yet by sunlight. She arched her back and ran her hands through her matted hair. The wind had fallen. The cool, washed air felt good; she lifted her face to it. She was amazingly alert and awake. The flowers, though dried and denuded of blossom, stood like talismans marking her path. She was beginning her way through them when the first strains of music, soft as a memory, sifted over the air.

She kept walking; the sweet music reached out to her, tingling and clear.

Then, with a sudden cold shudder, she realized: the harpsichord in the shadows! Fingers—invisible fingers playing the dusty, neglected instrument? Impossible! She paused and looked carefully round. The silvery chords seemed to slow, linger in the air, and then fade out altogether, until all about her was still.

At last she moved forward along the path again. She had heard what she had heard, and there was no explanation for it. Surely the sleeping man, injured and exhausted, with one useless arm, had not risen to play that harmonious, haunting tune. Anne did not feel afraid. Rather she felt a gentle presence which seemed to move with her as she walked through the slumbering gardens, strangely refreshed and at peace.

6

$\mathcal{A}$nne awoke late, feeling disoriented and drugged with fatigue. With some misgivings she walked out of her room into the midday household. Would things be going on about her as usual? Or would each person she met pause in horror or astonishment or, worse, excited accusation concerning the events of last night?

No one said a word to her. It seemed impossible that not one person could know. Rowena even appeared pleased that Anne had slept late and pampered herself a little for once.

"Though sadly, lass," she admitted, "you don't yet look rested to me. A little peaked about the mouth and eyes. A week's worth of late mornings might do."

Anne listened, wide-eyed and speechless—grateful, but feeling even more isolated. And her concern for Dougall ran like a torrent through her. How could she still it, mould it into the proper, ordinary functionings of an ordinary day?

It had been necessary for her to leave the door to the heather cottage unlatched so that the concealed man might leave at his will. She longed to rush back there this moment to see if he lingered or if he had made it safely away. But, of course, she dared not. In caution, she even avoided the direction of the gardens, lest she inadvertently draw attention there. She would return that night late, after all were in their beds, and secure the cottage again. The only risk she was taking was that Gareth might notice the one missing key from his bunch.

The hours of the day which were left to her seemed empty, and they passed at a torturously slow pace. She needed far more sleep, but she could not go back to bed, and she had little heart or energy to do anything else. Midafternoon, walking out of the laundry with a determination to retreat to the library to rest and read, she paused. She had heard a definite sound, a long, harsh scraping sound which seemed to come from the low dark passage which led from the laundries to one of the oldest portions of Ravenwood House. She heard it again, and then the definite measure of footsteps. She took a step forward. She ought to investigate this new intruder, yet she recoiled from the prospect. The steps grew louder and bolder, coming nearer and nearer. She moved back against the shadowed stone wall and shivered at the cold touch of it.

He saw her before she saw him, before she realized who he was. "Anne, whatever in the world—" His hands, warm and firm, closed on her shoulders. "Are you hurt, lass?"

She must have looked dazed still, but unharmed, for he pulled her closer. "You were coming to meet me, in the ancient halls where secret trysts have taken place."

"You're filthy, my lord, and unshaven, and . . ." *And home!* she wanted to say. But instead she lifted her face and returned his kiss with an enthusiasm that made her long for more when he took his lips away.

"Come, Anne, this place is dank and damp. I'm in need of the warmth and the light."

"I'm sure you are," she murmured, thinking of the wounded man who had come in at another dark, low door just hours before.

Will he tell me what has happened? she wondered, following him, pulled by his hand. *Will he tell me something, some part, or pretend nothing has happened at all?* She wondered with some interest, though another voice inside her said: *No matter. He is home again, safe and sound.*

It was not until later, when she dressed for dinner, that Anne noticed her loss. The Lockhart ring! It had been on her finger; she had not removed it. Where could it possibly be? She closed her eyes, trying to remember. She had played with it, thought of it, with reassurance, while she sat and waited for the queen's men to come. Had it worked itself from her finger somewhere between here and the gardens? She retraced all her movements in her mind: *caring for the gentleman!* It must have slipped off during the washing of his wounds. She did not usually work with the ring on her finger, because it fit loosely and she always feared she would lose it.

"Anne, are you ready to walk down with me?" Dougall stood in her open doorway. She straightened and smiled. "I'm ready." *He is a good-looking man, really,* she thought. *I like his eyes and the bold thrust of his chin and his air of energy and purpose, softened by the kindness that's in him.*

She walked with him down the long stairs. *I can yet steal out later,* she told herself. *Dougall is weary and will sleep soundly. I can search for my ring before locking the cottage. Surely I will, I must, find it there!*

Conversation during the meal was light and pleasant. Dougall made not the slightest reference to his activities of the past few days. He seemed interested in her: the improvements she and Hector Ewen were suggesting, the state of her health. Christmas, then the new year would come soon, and shortly after that the child would be born. Anne was never to know what Dougall might have told her, later, alone in the library. Before the meal was quite finished Gareth marched into the room. He bent low beside Dougall's chair and whispered something into his ear. His face was dark and his eyes avoided her. She felt her breath catch in her throat, and when Dougall threw her only a quick glance and, pushing his chair back, began to excuse himself, she felt a film of perspiration break out on her forehead.

"Gareth's business concerns me," she said, "so he had best state it here, with both of us present."

Making this bold request drained all her nerve. She waited, watching the play of Dougall's features—why were his expressions so impossible for her to read! He lowered himself into his chair. "The lass is right. State your case, Gareth." His words were a growl; he was already provoked and would not meet her eyes. How much had Gareth's whispered message revealed?

"The heather cottage has been disturbed and the key is missing. It even now stands unlocked, and there are signs of—"

Dougall interrupted his factor with an impatient wave of his hand. "Do you know anything of this, Anne?"

"I had not determined whether to tell you or not, Dougall," she began. Then, leaning a bit forward in her chair, she added, "Especially since you have not seen fit to disclose any of your activities to me."

He turned to face her, all interest. Anne continued, "A gallant group of the queen's men came calling in the wee hours of the night, sir. They were most anxious to see the laird."

Dougall clenched his fist and brought it down against the table so that the crystal and china rattled. "I ought to have known! But what's for it? What could I have done? I was helpless right then!" He glanced up at Gareth, as if for confirmation, and the man nodded grimly. "Did they search the house, Anne?"

"'Twas their intention to do so, and they desired it greatly. But I would not receive them."

Both men stared open-mouthed at her. She felt suddenly angry with them, and with all men who played their little-boy games with people's lives.

"I told them no, bluntly. I had no intention of allowing them their way in the matter."

"Well, I'll be . . ." Dougall nearly laughed. "Entirely unexpected; shocked them, I suppose." He was leaning forward on his elbows; his eyes seemed excited, but his forehead was creased. "Did any of them threaten or harm you or—"

She shook her head at him. "No! But you may believe it was most unpleasant, and so was what followed." She told him of her visitor. Deciding to hold nothing back, she retraced the events of the previous night. She could feel their amazement and sense Gareth's reluctant respect.

"Why did you hear none of this, man?" Dougall roared at Gareth.

The man shrugged his broad shoulders. "I know not, Dougall. I retired to bed much as usual, after taking a pint with Jimmy MacKenzie—" Both men stared at each other.

"MacKenzie drugged your ale! This was planned by someone who knew well our actions." Dougall pounded the table again. "But who, Gareth, who?"

Anne had told her listeners of everything except the earliest incident, the first visitor of the night, who had brought her warning. Thinking back on it now, forgetting the conversation at hand, she was startled to hear Dougall mutter, "The fool! MacDonald should never have come here, no matter his need! When I think what might have happened. He endangered all—" He stopped himself, turned sharply, and held his hand out, palm up. "The key, Anne."

She blinked at him. "What?"

"The key to yon cottage. I'll lock it and throw the key in the river this time. I'll burn the place! Perhaps I ought to, or have the men tear it down."

Anne pushed her chair back and stood to face him in her amazement. "What nonsensical ravings are these?"

"Why did you think of the cottage?" he hissed. "Why did you disobey my orders? What might they have done if they'd caught you

harboring a Jacobite!" He shuddered visibly. "And traipsing about in
the night, wet and chilled, hefting heavy buckets—what of the safety
of the child?"

"I did not endanger your child nor myself," she snapped back at
him, "in helping one of your friends."

"If only you were not so bold, Anne!" He thrust his outstretched
hand closer. "Give me that key."

She dug it from her pocket and threw it across the table. It slid
with a loud scraping sound, then fell with a reverberating ringing
upon the floor. "Have the key and the cottage—have your gentlemen's
affairs and intrigues! I've no use for the lot of you!"

She turned and rushed from the room. Not until much later did
she remember the ring, and then she cursed Dougall anew. What
great, ignorant louts men were, be they commoners or kings! She had
thought Dougall would fuss over her, praise her. But this absurd anger,
this stony rejection—where did it come from? And why? Why did life,
merciless and fickle, toss her about this way, between two extremes?
She kept herself aloof from her husband all of the next day. If he were
to come to apologize to her, explain his strange behavior, perhaps . . .

Late in the afternoon Rowena announced that a visitor awaited her
in the small front parlor. "What visitor did you admit without my
knowledge?" Anne questioned.

"A person I believe you should see, ma'am," Rowena replied, unruffled.

When Annie entered the room she was surprised to see an old
woman, diminutive and white haired, sitting and waiting with placid
patience, her hands clasped in her lap. She had fine slender hands,
Anne noted, which had escaped much of the gnarls and spotting of
age. When she saw Anne the woman smiled a slow, gentle smile and
spoke before Anne had a chance to either welcome or question her.

"I hope I do not disturb you, mistress, and I hope I do not make
too bold." She had a voice as light and airy, as sweetly pitched as a
child's. Anne nodded and moulded her face into a smile. "Come sit
here, dearie," the old lady invited, patting the chair close beside her.
Anne did as she was bade. "I'm Mary Forsythe," the woman said simply, "and I've brought along some wee gifts for the bairn."

She lifted a tied bundle at her feet and opened it to reveal the
sweetest of tiny shirts and knit stockings, bonnets and snowy white
gowns, some lace trimmed, some edged with bits of colored ribbon, so
soft, so new. As Mary spread the gifts out on her lap and Anne's, Anne

held one up to her cheek. "This is too generous! These are exquisite," she marveled. "Did you sew these with your own hands? This is too kind." *I do not even know you,* her eyes said.

But the old lady simply patted her hand. "I've been waiting for this pleasure these many years, waiting and storing, my dear, since my own lass was your age."

Anne stared back at her.

"Of course you don't understand." The woman leaned back with a sigh, fingering the small garments idly as she talked. "I nearly came to live in this house once myself," she began. "That was many years ago, when my Gracie was a girl of eighteen and yon laird was a young man himself, of scarce twenty and three." Her voice was smooth, her words sane and altogether normal. But the things she was saying pierced through Anne's heart, and she, too, leaned against the chair for support.

"She was a rare girl, my Grace, and they were so happy together. He built the small heather cottage at the end of the garden for her, did you know? How many glad hours the two of them spent there. They were to be married in June. But that winter came a terrible plague through the village and Gracie took ill." A dull pain coated her eyes for a moment. "We buried her two weeks before her wedding day."

Anne shuddered and closed her eyes. "I finished her marriage frock and we dressed her in it. She was still a sight to behold, though lying so stiff and pale . . . well . . . 'tis past. 'Twas a long time ago now."

It was a sweet sorrow that softened the old woman's voice. Anne found the courage to open her eyes. The clear old eyes smiled into hers. "But now you are here, my dear, every bit as pretty as Gracie was. How happy you've made the good laird, and he still a young, vibrant man. Is that not right, lass?" A small twinkle brightened her eyes. "And now a child. What a blessing! Forgive me for wishing to share it. Perhaps 'twas selfish and vain."

Annie reached out for her hand. "No, 'twas loving and gentle of you. Thank you for sharing your heart with me, thank you for this loving labor." She touched the small frocks, smoothing them with her hand.

Mary Forsythe seemed pleased. They chatted a bit longer, the vague pleasantries of most conversations, then Mary left, making no promises, though Anne had entreated her to return.

Alone in the room, Anne examined the exquisite handwork again. Perhaps she ought to feel jealous, perhaps she ought to feel threatened.

But, strangely, the sweetness remained, and with it a new awareness of the man she had married. So Dougall had loved before. So there were things buried in his heart that no eye had seen.

When she realized that Rowena had quietly entered the room, she asked, without looking up, "Did you know Grace during the time she was here?"

"Yes, I did."

"Was she as lovely as her mother said?"

"My, yes, every bit. But no prettier than you, lass."

Annie colored; that had not been the purpose of her question. "Where does her mother live now?"

"In one back room in a wee bit of a cottage belonging to other folk. 'Tis a shame. All her children gone, and no one to care for her. One son died in the king's service, another left these parts years ago." Rowena shook her gray head, then came close and marveled over the baby clothes with Anne. "Mark you how small and even her stitches are. Few anymore sew like that."

As Rowena pattered out Anne gathered courage to ask the question she wished she had thought of while Mary Forsythe was still there.

"Was Grace Forsythe musical, Rowena? Did she play the harpsichord?"

"She could both sing and play, Anne. She could coax out music that only an angel could."

Anne closed her eyes and remembered the sweet, haunting tune she had heard in the starlight and the gentle feeling of peace it had seemed to bring. Yet now the pricklings of jealousy stung her. The heather cottage, sacred to Grace and her memory—forbidden to Anne! Carefully she gathered the infant clothes and walked up the stairs. There were many strange and weighty matters that sat like heavy shadows upon her mind.

his is nonsense!" Anne's hand trembled and her voice rose. "Who prepared these charges? I demand to know."

"The lad was seen prowling about the place the night of the raid, ma'am, and was spied on the roadway as well. And how many, I ask, traveled safe on the roads that night?" Gareth swallowed nervously, but his voice was bold and pressing. "He has been heard to say that he holds not with civil disobedience or schemes against state. And *some-one* warned the king's forces, that's certain. We've every reason to be-lieve—"

"You are fools, all of you! Gregor MacBain came here to warn me."

Gareth raised an eyebrow, and his look unleashed fury in Anne that stirred her cold fears. "Who accuses this man?" she demanded.

"The names are all there on the paper. William Smythe, Allan MacNab, old Rab of—"

Anne made a sound of disgust and crumpled the sheet in her hand. "I have power to dismiss these charges. This is a citizens' com-plaint; singly and jointly the laird and I hold power to dismiss charges made in his name, and you know it. I am dismissing the charges now."

Gareth glared at her, but she was too angry to care. These days they hanged men for less. She trembled to think of Gregor, innocent and loyal, placed in such danger—and on her account. She let the paper fall from her hands. "*You* are dismissed now, Gareth, as well."

He stalked from the room, and Anne sank back in Dougall's big chair and waited, wondering how long it would take the factor to tell his master what had just happened and how quickly her husband would consequently come to confront her. She clenched her hands in her lap, set her jaw, and waited, while the afternoon waned and the lengthening shadows sucked all warmth from the dimming light. From where she sat she could see the gardens stretching into the distance, exposing in their winter nakedness the small thatched cottage which harbored the hopes and dreams of a man she scarce knew.

She heard his approach, the scrape of his boots over wood, and sat up straight to receive him. When he entered the room the first thing he did was bend down and retrieve the paper and smooth the wrinkled mass in his hands. "What's this, Anne? Do you defy these charges?"

"I scoff at these charges, my lord!" She must keep her voice slow. Slow and ever so reasonable. "You forget, Dougall, that I know this man well. He would never stoop to do that which he is accused of here. You misjudge him sorely."

"Men saw him—"

"Angry men, restless for revenge, pounced on him as a scapegoat. He came here to warn me that night. Yes, he traveled the roads, but he risked his life to do so, that mine might be safe."

"Is that all he did, Anne?" It was a cold accusation he hurled at her.

"I am two months away from bearing your child," she returned. "Do you think you need ask?"

"If 'twere any other man accused you would not bother to save him."

"Oh, but I would! You know not the common folk and our fierce loyalties! If 'twere any other man *you* would accept my word and not mistrust me."

Dougall hurled the missive onto the desk as though it burned to his touch like live coals. "You love him still! You have never stopped loving him. Admit the truth of it, Anne!"

"What difference does it make who I care for? What difference to you—who still love a dead girl more than the woman who carries your child!"

Her words were a blow. His face paled.

Anne continued, "How boarish of you to accuse me! Your heart is buried with her. I am a convenience, a means of procuring an heir!"

"Anne, in heaven's name!" His face had turned ashen.

"Tell *me* you didn't love Grace."

"I loved her truly. I wished I could cease to exist when she died. But you! You are—" His voice broke in pain. But Anne's own pain blinded her.

"Now you wish the man I have loved to die, too. Is that not so? You are miserable and you wish—"

"Anne, don't!" He grabbed for her, but she pushed back the chair, struggled to her feet, and slipped past him.

"I love you, Anne. I've tried so often to tell you. I've wanted . . ."

His voice faded; she lost his words as she fled the room and ran as swiftly as her awkwardness would allow her to the only haven she knew. He would catch her if she tried the stairs, but she felt that the gardens, cold and empty as they appeared, were hers. On a bench behind a low wall, set in a bed of dried lavender, she sank into a heap of misery and hot, choking tears. She cried until the very strength of the sobs forced her to stop and catch her breath. Her head ached, and her watery sight was blurred. The lengthening shadows were cold and she had no shawl, no covering at all.

Light and silken, like soft, scattering petals, the melody came. Anne put her hand to her throat and breathed deeply. Sweet on the calm evening air came the notes that no human hand played. Anne closed her eyes, and from her heart came an answer she had not looked for before. "He loves me." She said the words out loud and, once spoken, they seemed to weld into truth. *Fear* stood behind his brusque, unreasonable behavior! He had lost once; he could not face the terrifying prospect of losing again. Behind her closed eyes she saw his face, heard his open laughter, felt the warmth of his hands.

It would grieve me if you wasted your life, Anne. Gregor's words, like a sudden light, filled her. *Waste my life, waste my life!*

Suddenly she knew. She stumbled to her feet and hurried back to the house. The sudden warmth of the indoors sent pleasurable chills along her skin, and the light seemed too bright for her eyes. Breathless, she reached the library. Dougall was there. He sat at his desk, his head buried in his arms, his whole body rigid and still. He did not see her, he did not hear her enter. In silence she reached out her hand and gently touched his bent head.

He lifted his face to her, and she knew even more certainly. Restraining herself with an effort, she said, "I loved Gregor once. As a child I loved him, and in fear I clung to that. But I know now, I know of a certain, 'tis you I love."

"Anne, are you well? Do you know what you are saying?"

She took a step closer and reached for the crumpled paper. "I have no doubts left." She bent, took up his quill, and signed her name to the paper, then placed it into his hands. "There is my faith and my heart. Gregor is an honest man. He will be able to contend for himself.

If he died, I would grieve. But I would lose nothing. Yet, my dear laird"—her voice choked—"if I ever lost you . . ."

She could not go on. She lowered her head, and suddenly his arms were about her and her joy was more wrenching than pain. He released the ruined paper from his fist and tore it into little pieces.

"I have my happiness. Bless you, I have my happiness!" His eyes were alight. "I have been so afraid!" A great shudder ran through him.

"Oh, Dougall!" She savored his name. "Fear no more, fear no more, please."

"The heather cottage," he persisted, needing to tell her. "I had a strange fear concerning it. I felt it would bring naught but sorrow to me. I should have torn it down years ago, but I could not bring myself to do so. And when you took a fancy to it, I thought it a bad omen! I was terrified that some cruel fate would repeat the tragedy."

"I know, Dougall." She smiled. "I've spoken with Mary Forsythe. She came here to see me, to bring gifts for the baby." His eyes instantly filled with questions, and Anne found herself wanting to talk, wanting to open the lonely paths of her heart to him. "I should like to bring her to live here with us. Might that be possible, Dougall?"

"If you truly wish it. 'Twould surely be no trouble for anyone."

"I truly wish it. I want her here where there is comfort and kindness. I want her here when our son is born."

"Son is it, then?"

"I think so. For some reason I feel it."

Night had draped the land in darkness now. They stood at the window together, truly together, for perhaps the first time, sharing one mind and one heart, and the sweet taste of faith, like a benediction, hovered over their best hopes and dreams.

Morag

1745

8

---

*I*t was a wild storm. There was no sky, no river, no mountains, only a landscape of rain, rain that blew slantwise across the drenched sky and hurled against the walls of Ravenwood until the window glass shuddered in protest and the wet, smoking chimneys moaned. Morag shivered with the damp chill, but she was not afraid. Like her grandmother, she had no fear of storms, but loved the wind and the stirring, passionate longings it drew from her. And, heaven knew, loneliness had become her best companion of late. Her father had been gone for months, fighting with Cumberland's army, serving under an Englishman and seeking the destruction of his own kind.

It had done her no good to remind him of his own father's loyalties.

"So Dougall came out for Prince James in the rebellion of '15 and was crippled for his efforts and lived in pain till an early death claimed him. I remember. I lived through it in my own way, child!" he roared at her. "I was his only heir, the only one left to comfort my mother when he was gone. I'll not be so foolish as to risk all, the way he did."

"What would Grandmother say?" she asked, more curious than taunting.

"Your grandmother was no Jacobite. She loved nothing more than she loved Ravenwood. She would wish me to do that which would harbor and secure her home."

Morag knew that her father spoke truly. She had known her grandmother well enough to remember her passion for family and home. Morag would never forget the time, shortly after her own mother's death, when Anne took her by the hand—her six-year-old fingers clasped in the soft but iron grip—and led her through Ravenwood House. They went into room after room, and in each one Anne would tell her some bit of history concerning it: "In your great-grandfather's time 'tis said King Henry slept here," or "Through that low door the Black Douglas entered, he who led the English a merry race and forced young Edward III to admit Scotland's sovereign rights." Her voice was low and controlled, but there seemed always a current of excitement stretched through it. Even as a child Morag had felt the force of that current. Not all the history she had heard was ancient: "Here stayed Mary Forsythe, who bided her last years in this house and was like a mother to me. In this lovely room, my dear"—Anne had patted Morag's small head—"your own father was born."

Morag remembered very little from that first round, but over the next years they repeated the ritual again and again. Perhaps her grandmother had realized that she would not always be with them, and she wanted the old ways passed on, the old legends, the old secrets.

The sudden pounding at the door startled Morag and she jumped from her chair, leaving the cozy library fire to rush into the hall, her heart pounding. *Who could be here at this hour?* She turned to see Thomas, her father's aged, gray-haired factor, coming from the direction opposite the sound. His pistol was drawn and his expression was unflinching. "Do not open the door to them, lass."

She stood for a moment undecided, but a sense of urgency swept through her. "Nonsense, Thomas, it is surely someone in need. 'Tis a terrible storm for any man to be out in."

She tugged at the door. The wind nearly tore it from her grasp, forcing it open wider than she had intended, and pushing inside the drenched, shivering human who stood on her threshold dripping, his sodden hat in his hands. An officer's hat, perhaps? Uniform of a Jacobite soldier—Morag caught that at a glance.

Thomas brandished his pistol; even his old eyes were sharp now. "We want none of the like o' you here. Off! Off this moment before I blow you to bits where you stand."

The man took a step back. He was young, his face looked exhausted, and he was soaked to the skin. His eyes met Morag's, and something within her relaxed.

"We were told by the village folk that we might hope for kindness at this house." He had a nice voice, of rich timbre, confident despite his misery.

Thomas's bristly eyebrows were pulled into a ledge over his squinting eyes. He opened his mouth to reply, but Morag held a hand out. "Hush. Hear the gentleman through," she ordered.

"I have a wounded companion," the man continued. "There are

four of us, ma'am, and we've been walking all day, trying to catch up with our company. Just a little food and a night's rest—"

"Not a chance of it! Do you think we are mad, lad, to harbor Charlie's soldiers?"

"Hush, Thomas," Morag snapped. "You shame me." She turned back to the young man, her mind racing ahead, considering possibilities. "I dare not put you in the house," she said. "But there is another place which might serve." She pushed the door shut, and a cold shudder ran through her. "Thomas, fetch my keys and Grandmother's heavy cape from the peg in the kitchen."

Thomas lowered his head and stood stubborn.

"At once, Thomas, or I'll lock you in the cottage with this man and his friends."

The old servant reluctantly shambled off, mumbling angrily under his breath. Morag turned with some urgency to her visitor. "I must be assured of one thing, sir, before offering you any assistance."

She had his attention; his eyes were respectful and amazingly calm. "My father is an officer in Cumberland's army." An involuntary reaction of surprise and dismay passed over his features, and the set of his mouth became grim. "You will hazard my safety and the safety of my house and betray my trust if you speak to anybody of the assistance offered you here."

"I understand." He stood up straight, almost at attention before her. "I am Malcolm Douglas of Moray," he said, "eldest son of my father, Earl of Angus."

Douglas. Morag raised an eyebrow. *A powerful name.*

"And I swear by heaven I would never do aught to bring harm to you." He spoke the noble words simply, which made the sincerity of them ring true.

"But there are more than just you. Can the men with you be trusted?"

"I will vouch for their honor."

Thomas shuffled up behind them.

"Very well, then." She wrapped Anne's long cape around her and tucked the ring of keys into a pocket. "Go to bed, Thomas," she directed. "And sleep untroubled as well. I am capable of handling this matter." She saw a smile, ever so briefly, touch Malcolm Douglas's lips. She walked with him out into the rain, bending before the slash of it. The heather cottage had never seemed so far a distance before. She had been there often; it was a place which held many fond memories for her. But the month was February and she had shut the place up for the cold winter season. However, once they were safely within, and the warm glow of a candle lit all but the most shadowy corners, the place seemed a haven indeed. At least the raging elements could not touch them here.

Malcolm Douglas escorted his companions inside and they placed the one who was injured on the old couch in the farthest corner. Morag remembered well the scene, described to her so often, of her grandmother hiding a wounded Jacobite in the forbidden cottage. It seemed so vividly real that she could not help but think of it now.

"Where are your thoughts, lass?" Malcolm had been watching her.

Uncertain, she lowered her eyes, then replied musingly, "You are not the first to be harbored in this recess." She glanced at the harpsichord in the shadows. "You bide in good company here."

The young man's eyes were thoughtful, but he questioned her no further, and insisted on accompanying her back to the house. He felt his way along the narrow path through the gardens ahead of her, in order to shield her a little more from the direct force of the rain. In all truth, she was glad of his help as she gathered food, warm, dry clothing, and blankets—things much too bulky and heavy for her to handle alone. She was grateful that the soldier's wound was not of a serious nature. The best she knew how to do was cleanse and wrap it with a generous sprinkling of comfrey, as her grandmother had taught her.

"Whiskey for the pain," Malcolm urged, helping himself to one of her father's large bottles.

In the end she did little at all. Malcolm bathed his friend's wounds, only allowing her to assist and encourage him. The other two men, both young, ate in silence. But, even after his friend was comfortable and resting, Malcolm refused food. "I will eat later, when you are gone. I have too short a time with you to waste it."

What a strange thing to say in that quiet, straightforward manner! "You will leave before it is light," she reiterated, going over the instructions she had given him. Then, unable to help herself, she asked, "Where are the prince's armies? What is planned, now that he has retreated from England and is back in Scotland again?"

"Some say we are fools to plan any encounter with Cumberland. There is a lack of spirit, and the men are sore and hungry."

"We continue to push north," one of the others added. "Some say we should take to the Highlands to gather time and strength, but there will be nothing left of us at all if we turn back now."

"Ours was the latest victory," the other boasted. "We beat Hawley's forces at Falkirk last month."

"So we heard." Morag smiled, but furrowed her brow unconsciously. "Why did the prince not push on for Edinburgh then?"

Malcolm shrugged his shoulders; in the gesture she read a hopelessness which disturbed her. "He wished to push farther, toward London, while we were still in England. But now that we have turned back, it seems no one knows where we are going."

A heavy silence swallowed his last words, and the little group sat under it, as one would sit under a weight. "And is the prince as bonnie and brave as one hears of him?" Morag forced a tight smile. "Gallant with the women?"

"Gallant with his soldiers, and patient as any man through all the privations we've suffered," volunteered one of the men.

"The women find him bonnie enough." Malcolm's voice was low and unhurried. "He does have an easy charm, learned at the French court undoubtedly, and a sparkle that lights his black eyes." He smiled at her, a slow, growing expression that reached out with the intimacy of a touch. This young Douglas possessed a dangerous charm of his own!

Under his breath one of the men began singing, so softly that at first Morag could not discern the words, but with each strain his voice grew stronger:

> May the heaven's powers preserve and keep
> The worthy prince in his Highland plaidie.

His friends joined with him, and Morag caught herself humming along:

> First when he came to view our land,
> The graceful looks of that young laddie
> Made a' our true Scots hearts to warm
> And choose to wear the Highland plaidie.

She sighed at the end of their singing, and knew it was not proper to stay longer. The men were tired and needed their rest. She bid them farewell, looking into their faces, so clear and handsome, so unlined yet by the struggles of life. *Will they lay down their strong lives for the sake of Bonnie Prince Charlie?* The question, like a terrible wail, shuddered through her mind.

She stepped out into the moonless night, drawing Anne's cloak about her. She felt a hand on her shoulder and whirled round. Malcolm Douglas had followed her. He stood perilously close; she could feel his warm breath on her cheek.

"I am overly bold, Morag Macpherson," he said gently, "but in times such as these, what choice does a man have?"

How can a lad woo with his voice this way? Morag wondered, nearly swaying with the strength of the emotions that surged through her. *How, standing here in the cold and the rain?*

With one outstretched finger he lifted her chin, so that her eyes were forced to meet his. "I have marched through many cities and many hamlets, and I have seen many a fair, bonnie lass. But you— there is something different about you. I have never been drawn to a woman this way." She felt the confusion, almost pain in his voice. He stroked her cheek with his hand. "May I return, when this terrible struggle is over?"

It seemed a shudder of terror shook them both, passing from the touch of his hand on her face to every inch of her frame. It frightened her deeply. With a cry she moved forward and lightly rested her head against his chest, overcome by yearning, and a pity that felt much like a mother's pity. She drew quickly away, close to tears. "Haste ye back! And God go with you!"

He caught up her hand and pressed it to his lips. Breathless, wordless, and weeping openly now, she turned from him and ran through the dark, shrouded gardens.

Once safe in her room she left the candles unlit, and stood in the thick shadows alone. Something had happened to her that she could not explain. She feared the feeling and shrank from it—and yet she wished it would never end. She made her way through the dark room to her window. She could not see the heather cottage from here. He lay there, this young, gentle stranger. Why should that fact comfort and warm her? With the first light of morning he would be gone again.

"O my bonny, bonny Highland laddie," she sang, her voice faint and timid.

My handsome, charming Highland laddie,
May heav'n reward and him still guard,
When surrounded by foes in his Highland plaidie.

The words had been written for the young Stuart prince, but it was another she thought of as she leaned her cheek against the cold glass and remembered his warm, gentle touch.

"How shall I return after such pampering, such comfort?" Her father bellowed the words in his characteristic way. Morag's heart ached to see him sitting warm and well fed at his own table.

"Must you return?" she asked, knowing the question was foolish.

"In three days' time."

Morag sighed and filled his wineglass. She had missed him more than she realized. At least since that strange night three weeks ago she had missed him with an emptiness which had not been there before.

"But I shall take supplies, ammunition, fresh clothes, and the spoils of your larder, lass, to help me along."

She smiled at her father. He was a kind, simple man, she had always thought, lacking the bulk and power of his father, lacking the fire of his mother, but endowed with a certain tenacity of his own, and a sunny disposition, which was certainly a legacy from Dougall. Her grandmother had learned to be kind. Though Anne had possessed the impulses of an angel, her fears, her passions, her convictions often got in the way. Even when Morag had known her, the fire was still the strongest thing about her.

"Think you not, lass?"

She looked up, startled, at her father's question. She had been totally lost in her thoughts. "I was remembering Grandmother," she apologized. "What was it?"

"I was saying that we have great hopes of catching the rebels. They're a sad, weary lot. Cumberland has a highly trained group of fighting men now. Once we force the Jacobites to do battle, we'll dispatch them in no time at all."

Morag's knees felt weak and she sank into her chair. "Do you truly think so?" she breathed.

"Cumberland's men have paper cartridges with measured amounts of gunpowder, while the Highlanders still use the old powder horns. The duke has trained his men to shoot three volleys a minute." Morag shuddered. "Oh, and he's canny. He's developed a new bayonet drill that will check the terrible impact of a Highland charge. He is one who does not live in fear of these rough, untrained men."

"This distresses you not? These are your own countrymen, Father—some you and I know by family and name!"

Geoffrey Macpherson blinked at his daughter, surprised by her sudden vehemence. "They do their country no service to take arms in a fool's cause."

"Your own father was a Jacobite, and for many good reasons!"

"I'll hear no more of this!" Geoffrey growled. "Don't distress me, lass, and for no good I can see. I follow my conscience, as every man must, and ye may thank me for it some day."

Morag was sorry. She thought, much against her will: *He, too, could fall in this conflict. I could lose him, and he could lose all.* She studied his face carefully as he bent over his food, for the moment intent on eating and unaware of her scrutiny. She had often wondered how her father had managed these long years following the death of his wife. He had fallen in love with Beth MacKenzie when he was only a boy, and had married her while they were both still nineteen. Anne had not approved, even though she had been married at seventeen, the age Morag was now. Yet in later years she seemed grateful for the marriage. "They had so little time, as it was," Anne would say. Beth was married at nineteen, a mother at twenty, delivered a dead child at twenty-two, and never well again until she died, a mere slip of a thing, two weeks after she turned twenty-six.

"Like Grace, so like Grace," Anne would mutter. "A sweet influence that just slipped away and left us."

It was not until shortly before Anne died, which was less than three years ago, that Morag learned the whole story concerning the dead girl her grandfather had loved. Anne grew in esteem in Morag's eyes in the telling. Morag was old enough then to judge the largess of a heart that could embrace a rival sanctified and set apart by the grave, and appreciate the dead girl's influence upon the man whom her grandmother loved. Anne, with her own hand, had lovingly cared for the mother of her husband's first sweetheart during the woman's last years. And she had insisted that the harpsichord never be removed from its home in the heather cottage. Once, Morag had grown bold and asked, "Have you heard the harpsichord often through the years, Grandmother?"

But Morag was not prepared for the response she received. After staring at her granddaughter with a thoughtful, considered expression,

Anne replied, "I heard it at those times when it was most seemly, Morag. I heard music the day Mary Forsythe died, and late, in a strong wind, the day we put your grandfather in his grave." She had then paused and studied her hands in her lap. "And there were other times. I heard it once just at sunset—three days in succession—sweeter than ever before in the gentle gloaming. On the third day your mother died."

Morag shivered at the unbidden memory. "Will you join me in the library?" she asked her father, as he pushed back his chair. "We could play a game, or I'll read to you if you'd like."

"Not tonight, dear." It was his usual answer. "I've so many details to see to before I return."

Morag nodded in compliance, and her father left the room without her. "He has no grace with women," Anne used to explain. "He isn't comfortable around them; never was. And he didn't live long enough in Beth's company to temper that."

Nevertheless, Morag had hoped that tonight, all considered, he might have relented. She walked alone to the library and settled into her grandmother's chair. But something within her was restless, and she rose with a discomfort that drove her to walk the grounds, though the brisk night air stung her. The crows, silent and graceful, dipped their wings, weaving through the last tattered ribbons of scarlet the sun left behind.

She avoided the gardens; there was nothing to see there this time of year. Beyond the gardens the heather cottage hunched its brown, mossy shoulders in a shroud of silence that Morag, at the moment, was grateful for. "You will not tell our secret, will you?" she whispered. *Of course not.* She heard nothing, but could imagine, the way she had as a child, shadows of the many secrets the cottage harbored rising up into the air, a faint gray film tinged with a golden glow, melting into the soft, enveloping cover of night.

9

---

*L*ong weary days stretched into long weary weeks. *Why is woman's role one of waiting, always?* Morag chafed at the tedium. Spring would soon soften the land, and then there would be labor in plenty for her young hands. But now, though it was already April, the weather was fickle and intemperate, with many days still that were wet and wild enough to chill a person to the bone.

Ravenwood was a prosperous house, thanks to Anne's organization and extraordinary vision. In her first years here as a young bride, she had implemented the most farsighted methods available, extending development and progress to her husband's tenants, so that the whole area thrived. And Morag, though motherless, had grown up in the happy contentment which she saw reflected in almost everyone about her. That prosperity was their salvation now, holding off the terrible privations many Scots were suffering in the holy cause of conquest and kings' rights. Armies were as indiscriminate as the elements in despoiling crops and cattle, rending the delicate shell of security and, with a clarion call of chaos, inviting poverty in.

We are secure enough—for now, Morag thought. But the thought was uneasy and brought her no comfort at all.

Morag was isolated enough that she knew little of happenings beyond Ravenwood. The village of Kingussie, her only avenue of information from the outside world, had not changed nor grown much over the last fifty years. Yet every few days, unable to help herself, she found some excuse to ride there, anxious for news, feeling a tension in the air that continued to build and tighten, like the tension before a storm. She felt that something must happen soon—and when it happened she must know.

As it came about, a runner brought her the news, and she awoke to the nightmare before a spring dawn awakened the day. *The armies are met!* She had no time for the dozen questions that came to her lips. The young boy on the lathered horse blurted out the essential facts, which were all he knew, and rode on to warn others. His tale was maddeningly sketchy and incomplete. Two days ago, on the morning of April twenty-sixth, in the marshy fields beyond Culloden House, Charlie's hungry and weary soldiers, less than five thousand in number, stood against Cumberland's nine thousand. The clans were broken, the men scattered in every direction, and the prince, already with a price on his head, had disappeared, most likely spirited by his men up into the Highlands for safety.

A battle. A victory. For the wrong side. The tension still sang through the air. And there had been much fear in the boy's eyes as he told Morag the news. She dressed quickly, after giving instructions that her mare be saddled and ready. She would ride to the village and see if more news had arrived. Highlanders never ran. She could not imagine pig-faced Cumberland beating and humbling them.

Before she had even made it down the stairs there came an insistent pounding at her door. Trembling, she flew and opened it—to half a dozen women, with as many young boys, all from the village, all faces familiar to her.

"Our men are pressed, pressed by Cumberland's soldiers," one stated bluntly. "The Butcher has given orders to kill every remaining Jacobite, even the wounded and helpless. And, of course, many who were entirely innocent and just happened to be in the way have already fallen."

Morag covered her face with her hands. *"May I return . . . when this terrible struggle is over . . . ?"*

"Will ye help us or no, mistress!"

"Of course I shall help you!"

Morag spent the next hour gathering everything of value the house could spare: blankets, coats, her grandfather's old woolen knit stockings, all the linen she could find, old hats and shoes. They had pulled a cart up to the front of the house, and now all hands piled it to overflowing. From the conversation round her as the women worked, Morag gathered that their destination was a stronghold secreted in the far crags of the Great Glen. Wounded soldiers were being brought there, and utmost caution was the watchword, else all lives, their own included, would be sacrificed to Cumberland's cruel order.

"I'm going with you," Morag said, as the last of the foodstuffs was loaded.

"Nay, lass, 'twould be most unwise," old Meg warned. "You had best bide here."

"I am young and healthy, why should not my strength be wanted? Think how many lives I may save."

"Let her come," spoke up a young girl, who appeared to be close to Morag's age. "She has as much right as we."

"Not so," spat another. "Her father himself is one of the wicked duke's men!" She began to make a low hissing noise far back in her throat that set Morag's hairs on end. Some of the other women and lads joined in.

"So, you will take my goods, but not my hand. Hypocrites!" Morag cried. "Dougall Macpherson was a loyal Jacobite in his time, and suffered for it. This house has served you all well. I am as capable, and as worthy, as the best of you. Who will choose to ride by my side?"

Hoping against hope that the mistress of the house meant the offer in a literal sense, some of the young boys volunteered. Morag had to smile at their joyful disbelief when she ordered several of her father's palfreys and older geldings to be saddled. When at last they set off toward the glen, they were a fairly substantial little procession, with young Sam Brodie, his red hair flying, riding the lead, and Morag and the lass who had spoken in defense of her taking the rear.

It was early morning yet, and the chill mists clung to the hollows, at times obscuring their path, which soon grew shadowed and deep. Conversation was difficult along the narrow, winding ways, but Morag dreaded being alone with her thoughts, and recoiled from the weak poison of fear they sent through her system. All the women, even her youthful companion, were timid in her company. So she rode most of the way shrouded in silence and the sunless gloom of the glen.

At length they were forced to dismount and lead their animals carefully around stone outcrops and through shallow rivulets that meandered off from the main burn that fed the mountain fastnesses. *Would the Sassenachs dare enter this severe, inhospitable landscape for the sake of cruel revenge?* Morag wondered, not understanding at all the motives which caused men to do violent, unspeakable things to one another. At last the cart could go no farther. Meg Shaw, who was the oldest and clearly in charge of the group, directed two of the lads to stay back and protect the abandoned supplies until men could be sent to assist them.

Carrying what they could in their arms, the rest of the procession walked on. Morag was weary, but did not wish to reveal this, so she stumbled patiently over the sharp, cutting stones, her back aching from the burden she carried, her throat constricted and dry. They topped a steep, buttressed rise, and down below stretched a valley, green and hazy under the thin mountain air. A solid wall of rock skirted three sides of it so that it sat like a bowl which had been cracked on one end. Through that opening the weary volunteers poured now, toward the gray thatched cottages that hugged the far sweep of rock, half-obscured, even in daylight, by the mammoth figures of dark, brooding pines. Morag knew not what to expect, but if someone would give her a glass of water and allow her just ten minutes to rest her aching feet, she would do whatever she was asked.

When they drew up before the low, quiet buildings, Sam offered to lead the horses to a half-finished but roofed-over stable and care for them. Morag gratefully gave them over to him. She had to stoop to cross a low threshold, and when she straightened and looked about her a cry of dismay rose to her lips. There were dozens of men here, seemingly stretched out where they had fainted or fallen; there was no order at all. Women who were apparently filling the office of nurses stepped gingerly round them, offering a drink here and there, a blanket, a rough pillow of heather, hastily packed and tied. Morag moaned and sunk against the support of the wall. The terrible stench made her feel faint and light-headed, and the piteous ravings and cries of the suffering men seemed a whirlpool she felt herself sinking into.

Meg, spying her, lost no time; she splashed Morag's face from a nearby bucket of water and held a glass to her lips. "Drink this, and pull yourself together, lass. Remember, you wanted to come."

Stubborn pride alone came through for her then. The first task Meg assigned her was a simple one: pass out blankets and clothes to the shivering, often half-naked, men. Most were filthy and stained from the battle and the long, pressing days of flight. Morag refused to put clean clothes on any who were unwashed, so her hands took up that task, too. When the linens and blankets were exhausted Morag found the hot, crowded kitchen and brewed huge caldrons of tea. Tea and bread—loaves some motherly woman was pulling out of an old, blackened oven. Morag felt her own mouth start to water. But, oh, how many mouths, how many empty bellies there were to claim a portion of those few loaves!

"Aye, 'tis but a pittance we have here," the woman said, in almost a scolding tone, reading Morag's thoughts. "'Tis a pity indeed, but some help is better than no help. That's the only way we can look at it, lass."

Morag didn't notice when darkness choked the valley. She worked until she thought she would drop. As the hours wore on she realized that night made no difference here; the men's needs did not stop. At last Meg pulled her away with a thin, withered hand, cold as ice on Morag's arm.

"Up the stairs, lass. No more for you this night. You'll be on one of those pallets yourself if you keep this up, and of no use at all."

She pointed to a narrow ladder leading up into a loft room. It looked uninviting, and Morag shrank back in distaste. "I need a breath of fresh air first," she pleaded, and slipped out before the old woman could tell her nay.

There were stars here, so pulsing and bright they stung her sore eyes, so close she felt she could reach up and touch one. She left the dark doorway and the stretch of pines, blacker yet, and stepped out into the sweet-smelling meadow. Gratefully she lifted her hot face to the clean breath of a mountain wind.

She saw nothing, heard nothing until a man's arms were around her, dragging her forward, lifting her clear off the ground. She struggled against his hold and his closeness, and the terrible things he was garbling into her ear. She did not realize that she cried out. But suddenly the binding pressure relaxed and she fell back, losing her footing and landing on the hard, rock-strewn ground.

"I meant the lass no harm," she heard her assailant growl.

A low, angry voice answered him. The tone was so thick with disdain that Morag shuddered at the sound of it, though she could not make out the words. As she struggled to right herself she felt a firm hand cup her elbow and lift her effortlessly to her feet.

"You are in more danger than you know, lass. Sad as it may be, you must not walk here alone!" He sighed, and his sigh carried sadness the way the wind carries sadness. "These men have suffered greatly of late and are not quite themselves. Perhaps you can look with some mercy upon what just happened—"

Morag cried out. She knew that voice! She could not see the man's features, but in the darkness she reached out for him. "Malcolm! Malcolm Douglas?" The words were a plea, and he answered them by gathering her into his arms.

"I never dreamed nor dared to ask this much of Providence!" he whispered. "What kind fate has brought you to this place, Morag?"

He gazed down upon her with pale eyes that, in the gloom, appeared too large in his gaunt, unshaven face. *He's just another scarecrow, like all the rest,* she thought. And she noticed, as they moved forward, that he walked with a terrible limp and as though each step pained him. She put her hand on his arm. "Were you there—at Culloden, Malcolm?"

He stiffened, and she felt a tremor pass over his flesh. "I was there, lass, but I do not wish to speak of it."

I have driven a wedge between us, Morag lamented as they walked silently on toward the dreaded hospital cottage.

"Does your father know where you are?"

His question and the nature of it startled her. "No," she admitted, "nor do I have any idea of his whereabouts."

"'Tis hard, lass. I am sorry." He lingered over the words, and she wished there was more light so she could see into his eyes. "You should be home, Morag, not here in this disease-ridden hovel. Your father will expect to find you there if he comes, and 'tis right that he should."

His words were a scolding of sorts, and they daunted her spirits, already tattered and wavering. She made no reply. "Go home, Morag!" There was urging in his voice now. "The madness grows more unbounded each day. If Cumberland's men should discover this place"— he shuddered again—"not one person would come out alive."

Something in his warning frightened her, but her feeling of wonder was stronger. He was not angry, only concerned for her, terribly concerned for her. His rough tenderness soothed and thrilled her at the same time. Questions came to her lips, but his refusal to talk about what he had gone through, what was still happening, forbade them all.

"Don't go back inside yet. Stay with me for a while, Morag." It was a plea he uttered, however well he disguised it.

"For as long as you like, young Lord Douglas," she replied solemnly. "For as long as you need me."

"I shall need you for the rest of my life, I fear." He murmured the words, knowing her ears could not catch his voice, but needing to speak his terrible, overpowering longing, if only for the mountain wind to hear and carry in silence away.

10

Morag would have been glad to leave, even if it did mean leaving Malcolm; the place was a torment for her, a constant test of her stamina and endurance. At the end of three endless days Malcolm came to her and said simply, "In the morning you are to go. There will be men to escort you, and perhaps in mercy you will send your cart back, laden again."

"Will you be one of the men?"

"I will not, but in time I will come to you."

Uncertain, yet knowing she must, she slipped the Lockhart ring from her finger. "Keep this," she said, "as a bond between me and thee."

He did not protest, but pressed the bright jewel to his lips. "I accept this with the most solemn, devoted feelings, Morag Macpherson."

"As I had hoped you would," she replied, coloring at her own boldness, but thrilling to what she read in his eyes as he looked at her.

Although Malcolm would not speak of all that had transpired, many were more than willing to; Morag had already overheard more than she wished to know. The battle had been clumsy and ill directed, and fought on low, boggy ground, unfit for Highlanders and their method of warfare. The English had cut down whole regiments: the gentle Lochiel was hit in both ankles by case shot and carried off the field by his brothers; Elcho's Lifeguards had bravely sacrificed themselves to hold the dragoons off for a vital ten minutes—long enough for the right wing of the Jacobite army to escape. After the battle Cumberland's men sat down and fed themselves on the field, strewn with bodies and gore, then continued to dispatch the Jacobite wounded without mercy, until, as one of their own put it, they looked more like butchers than soldiers, their white breeches splattered with blood. "No quarter for the rebels" meant that many innocent country folk, unfortunate enough to live near the scene of the battle, were sacrificed to the spirit of murder. They were killed in the fields while they worked, or even within their own homes—killed simply because they were there, simply because they were Scots. Clansmen pathetically sheltering themselves in rude huts were burned to death, their sanctuaries turned to cruel death traps despite their piteous pleas. Prisoners were herded out to empty fields, lined up, and shot, then bashed in the face by the butt ends of the soldiers' guns, just in case they still lived. On and on the horrors rolled like cold black waves over her, until Morag begged the men to cease their telling, for mercy's sweet sake.

She and Malcolm stole every minute they could snatch away and luxuriated in one another's company. He had first come here wounded and weary himself, but had gone back twice, scouting the ancient paths and byways for those more in need than himself. Now that Morag was ready to leave him he was vague about his own plans, and fear for his safety began to consume her.

On the morning of her departure Meg awakened her early, while the sky still wore night's shroud. But the birds, day's first harbingers, sang to her, and light broke over the far hills with their song. As Malcolm lifted her onto the palfrey Sam had saddled for her, he kissed her farewell, a lingering kiss that drew all her longings, like sweet nectar, to season her lips.

She rode home. Her mind was grateful and happy to do so. But her heart lingered, in desire and imagination, beside the young man who stood tall and silent upon the dark mountain to face the new dawn alone.

He had no welcome for her. He watched her enter the house as he would have watched a stranger. She spoke to him gently. "Father, come sit in the library and talk with me, please."

He would have none of her reasonings, none of her explanations.

"Where are the geldings and palfreys that were taken from my stables?" he demanded. "Where are my potatoes, where is my grain—"

"Father, stop it!"

"You romantic little idiot! Why must you always hazard what I strive to keep and protect?" His face was livid, his eyes hard.

"I believed it the right thing to do. You would agree, if you could see what I have seen."

The sound he made stopped her cold. "I have seen that which would turn your hair white and freeze your heart in your breast for the remainder of your life, lass."

Looking into his eyes, she believed him. "Then have mercy, Father!" she cried.

He walked away, out of the room, but she knew she had won when he had no reply to hurl back at her. Even yet, he softened slowly, though Morag exerted a determined patience with him. Had they not both been blessed? He had survived the whirlwind; though he had been terribly wounded, he was home with her, safe. Ravenwood was intact and, hopefully, unthreatened, since her father possessed the fortunate wisdom to fight on the winning side.

Such reasoning helped Morag, but was of no good to her father. He had a terrible hole carved out of his side, which some surgeon had clumsily sewn for him. The stitching was red and sore, and in some places infected. He required constant care and was in more pain, she guessed, than he would admit to her. He suffered great swings of mood. Sometimes, with terrible coldness, he would withdraw himself from her and refuse to speak or respond at all. Other times he would bellow for her, his voice echoing through the sad corridors of the old house so that Morag, rushing to him, would mutter, "Grandmother, help me! What would you have done with this man? How I could use even a touch of your wisdom now!"

They managed clumsily through the days until the days became weeks and Morag was able to notice improvement that appeared stable and promising. But no word from Malcolm came. Sometimes at night she would be awakened from dreams of him, or cry out in her sleep. Her days were busy overseeing the planting of her father's fields and the care and protection of what livestock had been left to them. In addition to her rash volunteering of her father's horses to destitute Jacobite soldiers sorely in need of a means of getting safely back to their homes, solitary bands of marauding soldiers had not been able to resist her father's herds of fat cattle and had made away with the bulk of them in unpredictable, sporadic night raids. Her father was stoic about the loss and said little, but his eyes smouldered beneath the bony ledge of his forehead, and he chafed against the crippling impairment which prevented him, for the first time in his life, from action in defense of himself and his own.

Morag knew, though she did not want to believe it, that Cumberland was systematically destroying all Scottish families of any power or consequence who had lifted their hands to oppose his father and defy English rule. She knew Douglas of Moray was one of these families.

She knew it, but her mind could not face this fact for fear it would shatter into a thousand fragments of pain.

Then, one sane morning, not bright and not stormy, a messenger rode up to the house. He was an older man; he wore no uniform, no distinguishing marks. He rode alone, and slowly, his eyes ever shifting and watchful. Morag spied him from the garden and, dropping her tools, rushed to meet him. Her grandmother's small silver pistol slept in the great pocket of her skirt, but she sensed, long before she approached him, that this man meant her no harm. As she came into view he dismounted and walked to meet her.

"Are you Morag Macpherson?" he asked.

"Yes. Why do you seek me?"

"Another seeks you, not I. One who stands in sore need of you."

"What riddles are you talking?" A terrible fear had gripped her insides. "Of what do you speak?"

"Malcolm Douglas has sent me to seek your assistance. He is hiding in the woods near here, but he needs help and asks if it is possible for him to spend a night in the haven—he said you would know his meaning."

"He is hurt in some way?"

"He was wounded by the duke's soldiers when they—I promised to say nothing! Will you help him, lady, or no?"

She glanced back at the tall house that loomed above her. Was her father even now watching her exchange words with the stranger? If she were to agree to help Malcolm, and her father discovered her, what would be the result? Yet she knew there was only one answer she could return.

But when she looked up at the stranger, she wavered. How dared she give him the key to the heather cottage and trust him? What if he were an enemy sent to trap her?

As though aware of her doubts, he thrust his hand into his breast pocket and drew out a small leather pouch. "He sent this so that you might know of a certainty."

She opened the pouch and pulled out the Lockhart ring, slipped it onto her finger, and put the pouch in her pocket. "Take this key," she instructed, loosening it from the bunch at her waist. "He knows the way, but beg him to wait until dark. I shall"—she pushed her hand through her hair, trying to think clearly—"I shall come to him the very soonest I am able."

The messenger bowed to her and turned to remount his horse.

"Will Malcolm be alone, or are there others?" Morag asked.

"None but himself, miss. I ride on my way as soon as I deliver this key and your message." He looked down on her with eyes that were gentle and sad. "God keep you both," he said, and kissed his hand to her before riding away.

Morag returned to the gardens; she must gather her composure before facing her father. His lack of mobility served her for the moment; once he was down for the night he needed assistance in rising and, therefore, would not be bestirring himself at every vague disturbance that came to his ears. And he usually retired early to bed.

Even so, the hours of waiting wore on, seemed endless. Small demands and annoyances jangled her nerves. She waited for a long while after her father went to bed, far longer than she desired, for caution's sake, and when at last she pattered through the dark house gathering things Malcolm might stand in need of, she grew startled at every slight sound.

Once outside, making her way through the gardens, she breathed freely for the first time since the messenger's arrival. In the darkness the flowers themselves were obscured, but their fragrance, delicate and delectable on the night wind, seemed to beckon her on. She saw no light in the cottage as she approached it, but the knob turned easily for her and she slipped inside.

He was there. She felt him, felt his presence before he spoke to her, before he found and touched her. She rested against him and was startled at how thin his body felt. He refused to hazard a light, and she could not see his eyes, but the taste of his kiss was soft with sadness and weeping, and in confused anguish she nearly shrank from his touch.

They sat in silence for so long that Morag felt herself growing drowsy. She was leaning against him, with his arms wrapped around her, though the right arm was bandaged and stiff. At last he spoke, his voice welcome to her ears after the ringing silence.

"I must somehow tell you, Morag. I want you to understand." His voice sounded tired, an old man's voice, and entreating, like a little child's. "After two weeks I rode home, careful to keep off the roadways, taking the woods and the fields, traveling mainly at night. I arrived too late. Gray spirals of smoke, as bitter as the smoke of battle, rose in the still air to greet me, and great piles of rubble, with nary a wall standing. In the midst of the charred rubble a rope dangled from a black beam, and dangling from the rope was my father—mutilated and grotesque, unrecognizable."

A great shudder passed through him, and for a moment he buried his face in her hair. "For some reason I had not expected—even from the Butcher—" He stopped himself. "I went in search of my mother and sisters. Jean, who is nearly your age, Morag, was taken off by the soldiers, I know not where. My mother sits in the cottage of the village seamstress who used to sew her fine dresses, sits in the corner all day and rocks, and rocks. The two younger girls are with her, and they help the seamstress, who is aged and bent now, and they care for their mother, but she pays them no heed. I spoke with her, I gathered her into my arms, but she did not know me. His voice rose to a pitch of sudden distraction. "She did not know me at all!"

Morag turned round and pulled his head onto her shoulder and cradled him in her arms. Even now the touch of him sent a feeling of well-being surging through her—a feeling that renewed her own strength. "My poor lad, my poor, poor lad," she crooned, shutting her mind to the horror, determined to hold it at bay.

At length Malcolm lifted his face, and she wiped his tears with her own hands. "Morag, I must go away."

"Away?" The word had a hollow ring to it.

"They are looking for me. I tried to return to the house—I wished to bury my father! But soldiers were waiting there. Someone must have seen me, or heard that I was back. They fired at the first sound they heard."

She touched his bound arm. "Malcolm, where will you go?"

"France. Many of the chiefs, those not in hiding, have taken passage already. Lochiel, I know, would receive me, or Fraser—they have suffered similarly."

"Will it be a dangerous journey?"

"It ought not to be, once I'm aboard a French ship."

"Unless you encounter an English vessel."

He sighed, and Morag began to feel herself become light and empty inside, as though all feeling, all sensation were being drained from her, for only in this numb, half-real state could she hope to survive.

Grandmother, she yearned, *come back, help us! You would know what to do.* She must have moaned or whimpered, for he bent and kissed her wet cheek.

"Do not despair, my love. I will come back to you! We must, somehow, have faith."

"How long?" Her voice was wooden.

"I know not."

"It could be—years!"

"Surely—no."

"I doubt it not. Why should the English relent when they have us under their heel?" The pain suddenly rushed back in, to fill the aching cavity, to fill every pore in her body with fire. "I can't let you go! I fear I will die if you leave me!" She hid her face against his warm neck. "Malcolm, please!"

He held her until the trembling was spent, until they both gathered strength to speak of the unspeakable, to face a life that loomed before them more horrid than death.

The black night gave way to the dawn without protest. Not until gray light, soft as a dove's wing, brushed the cottage windows and gave promise of more light to come did he rise to leave. She met him in the garden path, where the dew was heavy and all about them was an unbroken stillness. And for the first time she was able to see into his eyes, deep endless pools of molten pain that burned into her very soul with a heat she wished might consume her and her own pain as well. *What will become of Scotland?* she wondered. *Is this a nightmare that is never to end?*

She walked with him to the edge of the woods, still inky black and filled with the moaning voices of the night wind. She must send him in there, into darkness, and away from her. Bravely she lifted her face to his kiss and let go of his fingers, which had been twined around hers.

"Haste ye back," she whispered. "Haste ye back, my love, and God go with you still."

He was gone. She was alone with the gray dawn and all the whispering and helpless ghosts of yesterday that were no comfort to her at all. She wondered if comfort would ever come into her life again. Or laughter, or love.

11

Somehow Morag survived, somehow she went on, day following day. Many things have power to kill, she discovered, but pain only cripples and maims a soul and will not let it die. She felt a stranger to her father; her terrible secret stood between them, and she knew she resented him because of his nature and loyalties —character-istics which forced the secret into hiding in the first place. Summer had come. Would planting and reaping, the age-old, life-giving rhythm, help heal the wounds Scotland had suffered? Were there men left to plow, and was there still land for the plowing? Could the dead be plowed under and rest, thus, in peace? What would grow from the blood-soaked soil over which the conqueror, with a heavy foot, had trodden?

A letter arrived by messenger one morning; it bore Cumberland's seal. Morag held it in her hands a long time before taking it in to her father. He turned it over himself once or twice before daring to open it. As he read, his face was a study, but fear was not one of the emotions that played there.

He tapped the letter on the desk and looked up at her. "Cumber-land has appointed me provost of the district." He sounded almost pleased.

"How dare you accept, Father? This is a position of judgment, meting English judgment upon your countrymen!"

"How dare I decline!" he bellowed back at her. "For heaven's sake, daughter, use your head! Better me than a Sassenach, for there are no other Scots in these parts whom the duke would trust." He leaned back heavily, already inviting the burden, hefting the size and weight of it. "There would be a chance this way to exercise justice, even mercy."

Perhaps, Morag thought, watching him. *Perhaps he would rise to the task.*

"I am to ride to Fort Augustus Tuesday next to make formal acceptance, learn my rights and duties, and so forth."

Tuesday next. That was in less than five days.

"Will you ride along? I should like the company, and would feel safer having you with me than leaving you here."

Companionship, or someone to wait upon you, Father? she thought, then instantly repented her unkindness and joined eagerly in planning the little trip with him. It would do her good to get away; she seldom even rode down to the village since her father's return and his heavy dependence upon her. She was stifled here, stifled by memories and reminders. The Great Glen in summer was always a lovely sight. With stirrings of real enthusiasm she made ready to go.

Every village they passed through was the same: choked with people—dispossessed, homeless people wandering the roads in an aimless stupor, often begging for sustenance, with nowhere to go. And the burned-out remains of once fine homes stood as ugly black scars that even the lush grass of the glens could not hide. Thin, hollow-eyed people walked the dusty edge of the high roads barefoot, whole families with children and babies. And riding smartly alongside them were red-clad Hanoverian troops, polished, well fed, and insolent. *So this is what Malcolm saw when he rode back in search of his family. This is what he endured!* No wonder his eyes had been half-crazed when he looked at her. No wonder he had begged her for a portion of pity and faith.

Only when they reached the fort and she saw the strength and scope of the enemy did the realization engulf her: *Fort Augustus is in the Highlands. A government army has penetrated the heart of a proud, ancient people. Can even the great clans sustain such a mortal wound and survive?*

Her father was to meet with William, duke of Cumberland, in the morning. They found an inn where they could stay the night. When they went down for an evening meal there were none around them but rough people: soldiers emptying large flagons of whiskey and asking for more; brash, gaudy women, camp followers mainly; and privateers who slipped past the naval vessels patrolling the west coast, in hope of supplying the English general with more attractive and less expensive goods than his own ships could provide.

Loathe to go up to their narrow, ill-furnished rooms, Morag talked her father into taking a stroll after dinner. His health was at last quite improved. She hoped the rigors and the politics of office would not undermine it again. Even in the soft light of the gloaming the camp town appeared dirty and ugly. The huge, noisy cattle yards didn't help any. The crowded, guarded pens had become a temporary marketplace for stolen livestock, herded in by the soldiers from every corner of the Highlands. As they drew nearer, Morag saw several shapes, stealthy, flitting shadows haunting the far reaches of fence line.

"Highlanders," her father explained, following her gaze. "Destitute families hanging about in hopes of a handout. I don't believe they'll find much mercy here." His voice was thin, his lips tightened into a line of displeasure. "This is a sorry excuse for a disciplined army of occupation," he muttered angrily. "Surely at some point enough is enough." He could no longer disguise his disgust.

Morag stopped. Approaching her was a small girl, not seven years old. She was dragging behind her a dirty, towheaded youngster who kept rubbing a fist into his red eyes and crying in great screaming wails.

"We'll find our mother, I promise, Donald! Hush yer terrible greetin'. You'll call the soldiers down on our heads."

Morag stepped into her path. "May I be of assistance, young lady?"

The girl blinked up at her, immediately wary. "I don't think so, miss. We've misplaced our mother, so we're walking about looking for her."

"Have you had any supper yet?"

The child lowered her eyes. "We're all right, ma'am."

"Here, take this." She pressed money into the cold little hand and folded the fingers around it. "You must keep up your strength, especially until your mother is found."

There were some decent-looking soldiers on the street close by and Morag turned to them. "Can you help us in finding these children's mother?" she asked.

One of them scoffed. "You can't be serious, lass. In this inferno of humanity?"

"She's probably run off with one o' them fancy cavalry officers who rode in here with prisoners yesterday, and forgotten all about these two tykes." His companions laughed rudely, and one of them winked at the little girl.

"Hush!" Morag hissed. "Shame on you all." She knew they would have been angry at her scolding and shown it if a gentleman and officer had not been with her.

"Mistress, for all we can tell she's been clapped in yon prison. Many hangers-on are."

"She'll have good company, what with the rebels rounded up yesterday," the first soldier boasted. "Mackintosh, young Mar, and the son of old Douglas we boys hung from the beams of his own house."

They went off into peals of laughter and rude oaths. Her father, growing impatient, moved to stand between her and the soldiers. "You'll get no satisfaction here, daughter. These children . . . well, there's nothing can be done for them here."

There was a terrible ringing inside Morag's head. Desperate, she pushed her father aside. "Are you certain of the men who were taken? You mentioned Douglas."

"That's right. With my own eyes I saw Malcolm Douglas march by, his hands and feet bound and a rope round his neck."

She swayed. Her father caught her, muttering his annoyance. The wide-eyed children drifted into the flow of passersby. "Where is this prison?" Morag demanded.

The only one who had spoken decently pointed it out for her.

"Come with me, Father. You must come with me this minute!"

Glancing an apology to the soldiers, he turned her round with a rough hand. "Come to your senses, lass. You're making a spectacle of yourself before these men!"

He led her away from the grinning soldiers and down a narrow, garbage-strewn alley. She feared she would faint at the smells in her nostrils and the ringing inside her head.

"Explain yourself, Morag. What were you talking of back there?"

She knew it would be impossible to put him off any longer; yet she needn't tell all. "They were speaking of someone I know. The son of Douglas of Moray."

"Douglas of Moray—who Cumberland's men hung from his own rafters. Yes." Her father's face had grown dark. "I knew the elder Douglas. As a young man he served with your grandfather. 'Tis a great pity—'tis a crying waste!"

"Will you help me save his son?"

"I'll do nothing of the kind, lass! I'm here in official capacity, by the duke's own orders. If I step even a wee bit out of line you and I many find ourselves in prison with young Douglas!"

"Then what's any of it for? If innocent people—the flower of the youth of Scotland—perish! What mockery you are engaged in, Father!"

She ran from his startled stare, ran in the direction the soldier had pointed, formulating her thoughts as she flew. It was not difficult to identify the prison, which appeared to have an entire contingent of redcoats guarding the crude structure. With only a vague notion of what she might do, she pushed past the outermost men, ignoring their ribald calls to her, and walked straight up to the door.

Here she was forced to pause due to the presence of a stout soldier with a rifle across his chest who stood barring the entrance. With a mingling of respect and friendliness which was difficult for her, she approached him. "Sir, my father is one of Cumberland's officers and now one of his provosts, and he has sent me here to inquire concerning several of your prisoners."

His return gaze was friendly and open. "Fair enough, young miss. Inquire away."

Morag thought it best to name more than just one, so she sandwiched *Malcolm Douglas* in the middle, feeling that her voice, her eyes, everything about her betrayed something as she spoke those two words out loud.

The soldier cleared his throat. "Those are all rebels of the first order, miss, powerful families. Who did you say your father was?"

She smiled and drew a deep breath. She must go slowly. "Geoffrey Macpherson."

"Related to Macpherson of Cluny? We haven't caught that old buzzard yet. Some say he could put up in the crags of Ben Alder for the next twenty years and even the eagles wouldn't find the nest he built for himself."

"My father bides yonder, gravely wounded in Cumberland's service, as loyal as you, sir, as loyal as any!" How acid the words tasted as she spoke them with purposeful relish. "As provost he has families in his district who make inquiries of him; he needs proper facts to make proper decisions. May I speak with some of the prisoners?"

She held her breath, but her heart beat so loudly she would not have been surprised if he had heard it.

"Not a chance. Pretty as you are, not a chance, girl. The prisoners are to be allowed no visitors. Ironclad rule."

You great dolt! Morag thought. She took a step closer to him, wondering in frustration what approach would most easily win him. "There are times when every rule serves best if temporarily bent or broken." He had trouble digesting that. Should she push him or give him time?

He looked confused still, and confusion brought out a stubbornness in him. "Break the rules when somebody else has to answer for it,
then, miss. Not me. Besides," he added, scratching up under the rim
of his cap, "these prisoner aren't bidding here long. They're due to be
shipped out."

"Shipped out?" Her mind was a blank page of incomprehension.

"For Australia. The penal colonies the crown keeps there. Cumberland gets a tidy sum for each head. Otherwise he'd simply hang the
lot."

She said nothing; she was unable to reply.

"Day after tomorrow they go, miss, up Loch Ness to Inverness.
Then they'll set sail from Fort George." He was looking at her more
closely now. "You all right, miss? You look a bit faint."

She must have said something. She didn't remember.

"Would you like an escort to your rooms, then? Listen, is this father of yours real? Are you staying somewhere in the fort with him?"

She touched the man's uniformed arm—uniformed, plump, and
well fed, while only steps away from her, chained and imprisoned,
hopeless and starving, bided the man she loved! "Thank you, I can
manage."

Fighting a wave of physical sickness she walked away from him,
stumbled clumsily along the flagstone courtyard as far as her weak
legs would take her, then sunk into the shadows, out of the sight of
men, and wept.

She had no idea how long she huddled there. When at last she
arose the stars were high in the sky and the streets were emptied, save
for patrolling soldiers. She approached one, not caring how he might
treat her, and asked him the way to her inn. He escorted her in polite
silence, and she wished she could thank him, but she dared not attempt to speak. She held his gloved hand between hers for a moment,
then turned and walked up the stairs. What she faced now she
dreaded far more than any encounter with Cumberland's men.

Her father had retired to bed without her help and was sitting,
propped up by pillows, reading by the light of one large candle. So it
appeared. But, of course, in actuality he was waiting for her. As soon
as he heard the door click he called our her name. She went wearily
forward and sank into a chair at the foot of his bed.

"I am waiting, Morag," he said, taking off his glasses and glaring
down at her. "I have been waiting a very long time."

Numbed with pain as she was, Morag realized that he was angry for his sake, rather than concerned for hers. The terrible loneliness within her deepened as she looked up and met his eyes.

"I went to the prison," she began bluntly. "I wished to see Malcolm Douglas, I wished to learn of his fate."

"And did you?" He squinted his eyes at her. She hesitated. "This is what comes of disobedience," he scolded. "You left your own home unguarded to run off and play nursemaid to dirty, motley rebels, and this is what comes of it!" He shuddered, and so did she. "You have shamed me, Morag, and I never looked for that from you."

"I meant you no shame."

He waved his hand at her with angry impatience. "'Tis done, just the same. And I am to meet with the commander himself, the king's son, tomorrow! What if some person of import saw your mad behavior this evening? What if the same is reported to Cumberland?"

"I doubt that will be the case." She spoke woodenly still. "I sincerely hope not."

Her docile manner disarmed him a little—enough for him to ask, "What of the prisoners' fate?"

"They are to be transported to the Australian colonies."

Her father swore under his breath, and she saw a quick flash of anger darken his eyes. "Well, there's naught we can do for it, at least not now."

"You could speak to Cumberland—"

"Daughter, have you gone mad? Ask favors for the sons of his worst enemies, as an indicator of the faith he might feel free to place in me?" He ran a hand through his thinning hair. "The timing is bad. Perhaps at some point in the future, perhaps . . ."

There is no future, Morag thought, with terrifying clarity. *In less than forty-eight hours he will go, and the future will go with him.*

"You look exhausted, Morag. Off to bed with you. A night's sleep will help."

She rose and left him. In her own room she shed her dusty clothing and slipped into a light night shift. But she could not bear to lie down. She paced the limited confines of the narrow chamber. In spirit she was with Malcolm, cradling his head in her lap, bathing his fevered brow. *He has no idea I am here!* she agonized. *That knowledge alone would sustain him,* she thought. Then, with a chilling shudder, *or drive him mad!*

She dropped down to her knees. Would heaven, in pity, heed her?

The time was so short, and she so entirely helpless. For a long time she remained on the cold floor, pleading. Though no answer came, a sense of peace settled upon her spirit and she was able to close her eyes and rest, to let go and allow tomorrow to take care of itself.

12

---

*M*orag awoke later than usual and felt dizzy and sleepy still as she struggled to rise. Her father had wisely requested that a breakfast meal be sent up to their rooms for them. By the time it arrived Morag was washed and dressed and more or less in order for the day, though her unruly hair still needed arranging.

"You look like your grandmother," her father remarked, unaccountably, as she walked out to join him. "Perhaps it is your hair. No, something about your eyes."

He ate with relish. Had he forgotten last night entirely? She swallowed a few bites, forcing them down, knowing she would need the sustenance. It was early yet. Her father's meeting with the duke was not scheduled until very late in the morning. If she could entice him out—perhaps a gentleman and officer in broad daylight could obtain admittance to the prison.

"Let us take the morning air, Morag. I'll go mad cooped up here."

She smiled acquiescence. As soon as she was ready they left their rooms and went down. The morning was fine, sun-washed and clear, yet with a cool lake breeze constantly bathing and renewing the air. Morag drew in deep breaths of it. Her father was interested in examining the cattle pens more closely, so they wandered in that direction. The prison lay close enough for her to still entertain hopes.

As they approached the outermost pens they became aware of a scene of confusion before them. Morag hesitated, but her father reached for her hand and pressed forward. He was wearing his uniform, as bright and starched as the others, and this got him past the sentries who held back a small, growing crowd.

"What goes here?" her father demanded in his roughest growl.

A young soldier turned to explain. "Bit of a scuffle with some Highland woman and her son, sir. Nothing out of the ordinary."

Just then a young boy darted out from among the soldiers. He was scantily clad and looked to be about twelve years old. "'Tis our cow, I raised her from a calf myself, sir," he cried boldly as the men who pursued him surrounded him in a narrow half circle. Morag saw that the boy had tight hold on a rope attached round the neck of a lovely fawn-colored milch cow. "You have all the rest," he argued, pulling the beast closer. "Without milk for the bairns we'll starve, what with Father dead and the fields in ruin."

"That is government property you are stealing." A tall officer stepped out of the circle and approached the boy. His voice, as he spoke, was a whiplash. "Hand her over to me."

"She is my property, like all the others you've taken. Leave me just her, and I'll go."

"Insolent whelp!" The tall man drew out his sabre. "Hand her to me, lad," he demanded again, "or be run through as a thief."

Morag didn't notice that her father let go of her hand and moved into the circle. But she saw the glint of sun along metal and watched the boy sink, soundless and limp, to the ground. Before he had settled she heard a high shriek, like the wild grieving of an animal, and a woman parted the wall of red and rushed to the child, bending like a scythe and covering his bleeding form with the plaid shawl she wore round her own body.

The haughty young officer replaced his sabre and kicked the still body with the toe of his boot. "Get them out of here," he ordered.

Before he could turn a voice commanded him, "Give the beast to the woman, and get this lad to a doctor."

The soldier lifted his head and looked round him with cold eyes. "Who dares to command the king's officer?"

Geoffrey Macpherson stepped forward. "I do, sir. Command you, and call you out as a cowardly beast."

The young man whirled at her father, taking in his uniform, his insignia of office. He clenched his fist at his side. "I follow the duke's orders in what I do, and you have no right to stop me." He kicked at the boy again, harder this time. "Get this rabble from here."

"You dishonor your uniform, sir. Mercy in this instance would harm no one and perhaps work us some good as well."

The officer eyed her father with such cold contempt that Morag, watching, shuddered. "You are a Scotsman, are you not?"

Geoffrey seemed to draw himself up a little taller. "Aye, that I am, and a colonel in His Majesty's army."

The Englishman, with cold deliberation, spat at her father's feet.

"It is impossible to be both at the same time, man. Every Scotsman is a Jacobite and every Highlander is a thief."

Her father paused. Morag could almost hear him grind his teeth, almost hear the thoughts in his head. Then, without reply, he bent over the weeping woman and, prying her fierce hold, moved her gently aside. "All the king's men are not beasts," he told her softly. "I shall see to the lad."

There was no warning. The sabre slid from its sheath and struck with the speed of a serpent. Her father's body shuddered once, then slumped across the dead boy and lay still.

Morag felt nothing. This seemed an unreal pantomime, enacted in slow motion before her. Her father would shake himself, surely, and rise, and it would all be some horrible nightmare. The young officer turned away. Hands reached down and lifted her father. Morag did not know that she screamed, not until a soldier clapped his hand over her mouth and dragged her away from the crowd.

"In heaven's mercy, lass, hush!" She struggled against him.

"My father!" she screamed. "'Tis my father that officer murdered!"

The pity in the soldier's eyes drove her mad. "Hush your wild screaming and I'll take you to your father. But you must somehow keep still."

Shivering with her efforts at control, Morag followed the soldiers, biting her white, clenched knuckles to stifle the sobs she could not hold down. In a darkened room, a hospital room she realized dimly, they had laid him out on a stretcher. Morag dropped down beside him. His white shirtfront was drenched in blood, and blood spattered his neck and face. She tugged at her handkerchief, wet the end with her tongue, and rubbed his face urgently.

"Bring a surgeon," she demanded. "Why do you stand there and do nothing?"

A man stepped forward, a man who had been standing nearby watching the scene. "The surgeon has already examined him," he explained, his voice carefully impersonal. "Your father is dead."

She bent over him. His eyes were closed, but he did not look peaceful. His features wore the impress of surprised horror. "What wickedness!" she cried. "What is that cruel officer's name? I want the name of the man who murdered my father!"

Morag whirled round like a she-cat to face her speechless watchers. Then suddenly everything blurred into a dizzy red swirl, and went black.

13

Morag awoke to such a profound silence that for a few moments she remained frozen, unable to sort out time and place in her head. When her memory of the morning's events returned she buried her face in the pillows, but the tears would not come. Then she remembered. *Not yet.* She must not give up now. If she failed, then she could give up, lie down and die where she was and let Ravenwood and the rest of humanity rot. But not yet.

She stumbled to her feet. Her head was still dizzy; even her sight seemed blurred. She found her grandmother's oval pocket watch pinned inside her breast pocket. Three minutes after seven! She had slept through the day. Why must grief demand all of one's energies, nearly consume one? She could still go to Cumberland herself. Is that not what she had determined, kneeling at her father's deathbed? He had missed his appointment. Had the great general heard of his murder? Would he bring action against the foul creature who mercilessly ended a noble life? Morag had a whole night ahead of her. She should eat—ought she try to sleep more?

She went to a window and drew back the curtain. A startled wren scolded her, then poked her slender beak into one of the crevices of the building in search of food. The sky was light; faint rosy streaks disappeared in the distance. People moved about in the courtyard below her. Seven o'clock, the watch had read. Seven o'clock in the morning? That could not be! How could she have slept through the night as well as the day? All those long, dreadful hours! Where was her father? Had they moved him? Where was Malcolm? The guard had said he would be shipped out the day after tomorrow. How much time had she left?

She bathed in the new water the maid must have brought in yesterday after she and her father went out for their morning walk. Who had carried her back to these rooms, and when? She began to dress hastily, but slowed herself. She must be composed, think clearly. What was Cumberland like? "The Butcher," he was called, but his men thought him a good general. Was he fair with his men? Clever—she knew he was terribly clever, also pudgy and soft fleshed, with eyes too small for his face. Yet her father had thought him not so bad. What should she do to assure the most favorable reception possible?

She arranged her hair carefully, the unruly auburn curls held back in an ivory comb. A touch of rouge to her pale cheeks—how terribly gaunt and pinched her face looked in the small mirror. Her gray dress would do; it was dove gray, a color suitable for mourning, but softly feminine still. She selected a pale rose ribbon for her hair, despite the mourning, for without it she appeared insipidly pale. She twisted the Lockhart ring on her finger. *Courage,* she told herself. *You will be able to do what you must.*

Despite countless fears and uncertainties that tended to unravel her resolve, at least she had something to focus her mind on, something to do. She almost welcomed her course of action, protecting her as it did from the eventual acceptance of the new realities in her life, which she had no desire to face.

She walked out into the street. No one turned to stare at her. Did she appear normal, then? She knew which building housed the general and his staff. She walked straight to it and entered. There seemed to be no one around. But she must have made enough noise to be heard, for a young aide came limping out and inclined his head to her.

"I am here to see William, duke of Cumberland," she announced.

The quiet-faced young man nearly smirked, but thought better of it. "Have you an appointment, ma'am?"

"In a way. Yes, you might say that."

"Please wait here, if you would be so kind." He nodded toward a chair and shuffled out of the room. Morag coughed and swallowed, trying to moisten her throat. The young man seemed to be taking a long time. He did not return. Her back, held stiffly, began to ache. An older man approached her finally. He wore a thin mustache and his hair was balding. Morag did not like his eyes.

"The duke is not here, ma'am. If you will leave your name—"

"I will wait." Morag settled purposefully back against the chair and folded her hands in her lap.

"I am afraid you do not understand, Miss . . . ?"

Morag did not like talking to him, and for some reason found it difficult to extend him the courtesy of giving her name.

"I am afraid *you* do not understand, sir. This is a highly important, highly personal matter. If the duke is not in, I shall wait." She kept her voice as impersonal as his, and her mind empty, lest pain creep in and betray her.

The man was more than annoyed now. "That is impossible, madam. I must insist that you leave."

He started toward her. *Will he throw me out bodily?* Morag wondered. The hands of the clock read nine-thirty. She had already waited for more than an hour. Surely they would not move the prisoners out yet. But then, they had a long way to go, and if there were schedules to be met . . .

"Miss? Will you follow me, please?" It was the young aide again. The older, angry-eyed soldier was nowhere to be seen. "Captain Williams will see you."

She followed him reluctantly down a long passage. Captain Williams had a desk in a dull room, otherwise empty. He looked up with a scowl.

"The young lady I told you of, sir." The aide poked his head in, then back out just as swiftly and forthwith disappeared.

"Now, listen here, missy," the officer began, "this is highly irregular behavior."

"I think not." Morag found herself despising him, and a cold, haughty manner came to her with surprising ease.

"Be reasonable, will you? The duke is not in attendance. We do not know when to expect him. So, kindly be on your way. You will be informed of the duke's return."

Morag did not believe him. "Do not be stupid, sir. Your commander expects me, and it is imperative that I see him." She turned her back on him and began to leave. "I will continue to wait where I was."

"You'll do no such thing!" he growled. "I'll take my chances with Cumberland when he arrives. You will quit these offices, my dear young lady, right now!"

He closed his hands on her arms and began to propel her forward by force. She struggled in his grasp and cried aloud at the cruel pressure of his fingers.

"Not so hasty, Williams, my good man. What goes on here?"

The soldier paused, and growled at his superior officer without thinking. "A lady, as you can see, sir—one of the good duke's *acquaintances,* which, of course, makes it sticky." He let go of her with a hard shove. "She refuses to leave."

He had pushed her nearly into the arms of the newcomer. She wavered a bit, regaining her balance, and looked up into quiet brown eyes that gave her the courage to say faintly, "I must see the duke, sir—now, this very morning, else all will be lost."

He rubbed his chin thoughtfully.

"Well, sir?" The disgruntled captain lingered, awaiting orders.

"Return to your duties, Williams. I believe I can handle this matter."

The captain shrugged and turned back to his office. The man with the kind eyes said, "Come with me, dear," and walked to the end of the hall. There he ushered her into a room much larger than the captain's, and nicely appointed. Feeling suddenly weak, she sank gratefully into the cushioned chair he indicated.

"You are not one of the duke's 'women', are you?" he asked.

Her astonished expression was answer enough.

"I didn't think so. But, haply, it has got you this far—to be mistaken for a paramour whom no soldier who valued his neck would insult!" He chuckled under his breath. "I am General Carpenter. How may I serve you?" he asked.

How may I serve you? Morag nearly broke down at the kind words. Instead, recalling her pride and her purpose, she drew herself up and began carefully. "My father is Geoffrey Macpherson, who served as a colonel under Cumberland in the king's army, indeed, suffered serious wounds in the king's service. Yesterday he was killed in cold blood by one of Cumberland's men."

The general leaned forward in his chair. His face held a piteous yearning, but his eyes snapped with fire. "I have heard of this most unfortunate affair, dear girl. I am sick with regret."

Morag swallowed, trying to ease the terrible burning in her throat. "Do you know the person who is guilty of my father's murder?"

The general slumped back heavily. "I know the young man, everyone knows the young man."

Morag clasped her hands so tightly that the knuckles whitened. "He will be punished, then? Brought to justice?"

With an audible sigh General Carpenter shook his head. "He is a favorite of the duke's, and he knows it. The brute boasts of his deeds!" The man across from her looked truly ill, and covered his face with his hands. "I am ashamed, for all our sakes, of his heinous behavior."

Morag leaned forward. "But my father was known of Cumberland—known and trusted. The duke had lately appointed him provost of Badenoch. In fact, my father was to have met with the duke yesterday. Surely the duke must have missed him and wondered—"

Confusion dulled the general's eyes. "The duke rode out of the fort before daybreak yesterday morning. He sent written word to your father that their meeting would be delayed a few days' time, until his return. I placed the note into the messenger's hand myself."

"We left our rooms early," Morag explained, thinking back with reluctance. "If the note was delivered, my father did not return and thus did not receive it." The constant pain was wearing her senses to a dull edge, yet now she had an object for her anger, something to fix upon. "My father came a considerable distance, through danger and difficulty, to accommodate the duke's pleasure. Why was the appointment not kept?"

The general smiled at her fervor; but it was a cautious and tentative smile. "For pursuit of a matter that supersedes all others. He received word that the Young Pretender had been caught somewhere on the coast of Skye."

"Rumor," Morag replied without thinking. "The Highlanders will never allow their prince to be taken, no matter how he has failed them."

The smile became warm, and tempered with a thoughtful expression. "I am sorry such a matter has brought us together, Miss Macpherson. I will personally make arrangements for your father's body to be escorted home with all due honors." His words, so quiet, so commonplace, brought the weight of reality crushing in.

"Aye, 'tis death and dying that has brought me here!" Morag spoke bitterly. "I had come to plead a favor of the great duke, a mercy I felt he might tender me, in justice—" Her voice broke. "Now there is no hope. When the duke returns, my cause will be lost."

"Whatever do you speak of?"

Morag rose to her feet. "'Tis the duke I must importune, no other can help me!"

General Carpenter rose with practiced agility, walked to the end of the room, shut the door tight, and threw the bolt to secure it. "You may speak freely now," he said, turning back to her. "And I assure you, my dear young thing, that fortune has blessed you this day. Cumberland would not weaken in sympathy to your cause, despite your father's cruel murder. *I* am your only hope, lass. And I stand here ready to listen."

"You have guessed at my difficulty," Morag surmised, her heart suddenly pounding against her cold flesh. "I want a life for a life."

The general regarded her closely.

"You have a prisoner by the name of Malcolm Douglas, who is to be deported to Australia."

"My dear, the wagons are loading, even as we speak! I was returning from the prison when I entered and saw you."

She leaned forward and grasped his hand. "You must do something! Please, in mercy, sir, save him!"

"He is the son of a notorious rebel—"

"Who is hanged and dead for his crimes. Whose house is ruined, his family broken and scattered! This man is worth saving, my lord!"

"Is he now? Is your word on the matter sufficient?"

Morag placed her cheek briefly on the broad hand imprisoned within her own. "I beg for justice. A noble and loyal life, who would have served the king well, I assure you, has been cruelly taken. Let this man live in his place!"

She dared not look up, but closed her eyes and prayed silently in the depths of her soul. She felt a soft touch on her hair. "Rise, lass, we must move quickly if we hope to succeed."

She released his hand. He had already reached for quill and paper and now bent and began scratching hasty words along the blank surface. When he was finished he signed his name with a flourish, then blew onto the ink to dry it, not risking the time to blot it properly. Hastily he folded the paper and applied hot wax, imprinting his personal seal.

"This will be sufficient. Hurry now, with good speed. I shall send a man to accompany you who will do whatsoever you bid him."

He threw the door open and stood aside for her to pass.

"Sir"—Morag drew his hand up and kissed it, holding it against her tear-moistened cheek—"I shall not forget your great kindness, but will live so you may never regret it." She drew herself up and looked into his eyes, her joy embracing him. "Myself and mine will pray for you always and hold your name in honor."

"Lieutenant Hill," he shouted down the long corridor. They heard the swift patter of running feet. He bent and pressed his lips to her cheek. "To bring happiness to such a brave, pretty lass warms my heart, which is overweary. Godspeed, Miss Macpherson."

Lieutenant Hill proved as good as the general's word. His horse was waiting by the door. He swung into the saddle and pulled her up in front of him, clattering over the flagstone courtyard round to the back of the prison, through tall iron gates which stood unhinged and open. With the wind blowing her hair across her face, Morag scarcely could see. Hill pulled up so suddenly that she lunged forward, despite his arm that held her.

"They're still loading the wagon, miss. You go look for your man; I'll take the general's orders to the officer in charge here."

Morag slid to the ground. A short distance away stood a large wagon, with high wooden sides. It was already crammed full of men. A thin trickle of a line trailed out from it: men in faded, tattered apparel, bearded or roughly shaven, eyes cast down at their feet. They shuffled forward methodically, as though unaware of what they were doing, as though they were only men in a dream. She walked slowly toward them, her eyes lingering on each for long moments. Where was Malcolm? She shivered at the sensation of watching the thin prisoners, shoulders hunched, eyes large and empty in their gaunt faces, who did not even notice her there.

He looked just like the rest of them. He had walked listlessly past before recognition sang like a song in her. She stepped into his path.

He stopped. He raised his eyes ever so slowly. He looked on her face as he would have looked on a spectre.

"Come with me, Malcolm Douglas," she said, not caring who heard her. "You are free to come home with me, Malcolm, my lad."

Joy pushed at the corners of his eyes, but he would not admit it. He shook his shaggy head, as though to dislodge her image.

"Lieutenant Hill," she called. He was right at her elbow. "Show this man your paper."

"He's too stunned to read papers, miss," Hill replied. He closed his hand over the knot of Malcolm's shoulder. "The girl speaks truly, man. You are free now to go."

She pulled him out of the line. It began, like a cumbersome snake, to toil forward again. For a moment her heart reached out and ached to save, to embrace every miserable shadow of a man who moved past her. Then she felt a touch on her cheek.

She turned with open arms, and he came to her, cradling his head into the curve of her shoulder, hiding his grief and his terrible joy. They stood thus a long time, while Lieutenant Hill waited at a respectable distance for them, and the heavy wagon rumbled out of the prison yard heading for the boats of the loch—packed to bulging, yet leaving one man, one trembling, ransomed rebel, behind.

14

---

*M*orag found Cumberland's letter propped on the dressing table in the room which had been her father's. The hard irony of it smote her like the sharp edge of a knife. She packed it in with his other belongings. Pity that Malcolm was too large to make use of her father's clothing. But she bartered one of her father's shiny red uniforms for some decent clothes for him to go home in. General Carpenter sent word that they should move out as quickly as possible. He had ordered an entire contingent to escort Colonel Macpherson's body; Lieutenant Hill was to ride at the head. At first Malcolm would have none of it; he was exhausted with fatigue and hunger, he was still coming back from the dead. He carried his lease on life, General Carpenter's pardon, in his breast pocket, and often he slipped his hand in to touch it and make certain it was there.

Not until they had cleared the Great Glen and left the dreary, crowded villages behind did the weight start to lift. Not until they topped a rise and saw the fields of Ravenwood spread out before them, with the blue river dancing along their borders, did the muscles in Malcolm's drawn face relax.

Ravenwood had never appeared more beautiful to her, and she drew up before the great house with pride. It was not easy for her to entertain the king's men in her home, but she would not send them away hungry. Hospitality, graciously given, was one of the sacred traditions of the Highlands her grandmother had taught her. She looked into the men's faces as they sat round her board eating. It was difficult to imagine them strained and set in battle, difficult to picture them covered in her countrymen's blood. They were men just like her father, and boys just like Malcolm. Or were they? Were they that less-than-human thing called *the enemy*?

Lieutenant Hill shook her hand when he took leave of her, then raised it to his lips and said gravely, "This is the most honorable, and delightful, duty I have been assigned since my arrival in Scotland."

"You have been an angel of mercy to my house," Morag replied. "God go with you and keep you."

She watched the long line of red move away and become a thin shiny ribbon as it wound over the far rise and disappeared from her sight. Turning back, she sighed with relief. She was truly home now.

"May I return after this terrible struggle is over?" Malcolm had asked her that first night. She trembled at the memory. He was here with her now. "I'll never leave again," she whispered. "I'll never leave the confines of this house and the safe village beyond."

They performed the rite for her father just before sunset. There was no time for a proper wake; the body had lain too long unburied. While the soldiers had eaten and rested, Malcolm, grateful to put distance between himself and them, had seen to the preparation of the grave. Young Rab, who had worked in her father's stables since he was a child, and David Gordon, Thomas's son, piped the body to its resting place. The old factor himself, his gray head bowed with grief, followed the coffin, which was carried on the shoulders of young men.

The strains of the ancient bagpipe music sent a solemn thrill through Morag, like the voices of her dead kindred moaning and sighing about her, thick with sorrow but vibrant with an ageless and undying strength.

The minister spoke a few solemn words—good, fitting words—before the open grave. Morag was surprised to see so many of the townspeople come to pay their respects. *The things they shared with him were stronger than the things that separated them from him,* she realized, watching their faces. Politics, power, and kings meant little next to birthings and weddings, illness, hunger, and death.

She bid the pipers play again as her father's body was lowered into the moist, narrow hole waiting to receive it. She shuddered before the terrible finality of it. "What a poor way to bring you home, Father," she whispered. "I am sorry indeed."

Malcolm, standing beside her, shook his head and replied softly, "No, no, do not grieve, lass. 'Twas a noble way to die. Your father does not begrudge it, nor does he lie ill content."

She knew he spoke truly. His words somehow released her spirit, and the pain which bound it floated away on the long, haunting notes of the bagpipes and disturbed her no more.

Alone in the quiet night, she walked the gardens with Malcolm, savoring the peace, the palpable absence of fear—that unwelcome companion who always before had walked with them. *Only land and love remain,* she thought. *All else counts for naught.*

"Malcolm," she said, "I hope there will be no wars and no killing when our sons grow to manhood."

"I hope better," he replied. "I hope that they will know the love and loyalty of a woman such as their mother." He kissed her, so tenderly that she wanted to weep. "And I hope our daughters may possess your secret, Morag—whatever it is that makes you so wondrous and fair."

His arms closed around her, and the fragrance of the gardens breathed over them. And, with the fragrance, a melody, light and sweet as a prayer.

"Grandmother!" Morag lifted her head, alert and listening.

"What is it, Morag?"

"Do you hear, Malcolm?" She tugged at his sleeve insistently. "The melody."

He closed his eyes and stood quiet for a moment. "Coming from the heather cottage," he said.

She leaned back against him, and they listened to the clear, liquid notes together.

"I have never heard it before," she marveled. "They are welcoming Father home. Grandfather, Grace Forsythe and her old mother—and my grandmother. I feel her most of all."

"Do you speak truly?" Malcolm asked gravely, deeply moved by her words and by his own feelings.

"Oh yes," she cried. "And this means that Ravenwood is truly ours, and we're not alone. We never were—we never could be, Malcolm."

Not completely understanding, but longing to, loving her, Malcolm reached for her hand. Beneath the high silver moon that lit their glimmering path they wandered the gardens, two solitary people who held all happiness, all promise, all possibility within their clasped hands.

Flora

1841

15

Can ye no hush yer weepin',
All the wee lambs are sleepin',
Birdies are nestlin', nestlin' together,
Dream Angus is harklin' o'er the heather.

Flora sang the song sweetly, sang it for the third time, though she knew the wee ones had already fallen asleep. She loved the taste of the words on her tongue, loved the way she felt when she sang them:

Dreams to sell, fine dreams to sell,
Angus is comin' with dreams to sell,
Hush now, my bairnies, sleep without fear,
Dream Angus will bring you a dream, my dear.

She savored the last words, letting go of the melody with reluctance. 'Twas a beautiful melody, but more than that, it was the song her grandmother had sung to her every night when she was a very small child. Morag was not really her grandmother, but her great-grandmother, ancient and wrinkled before Flora had opened her eyes to the light of day. This place, Ravenwood, had been Morag's house. She had buried a murdered father, an infant daughter, and a husband here, biding past the memories of her own life to see both her son and her daughter let go of living before she did.

Flora rose slowly and bent to kiss each soft cheek just once more before tiptoeing out of the room. *How I wish you were mine!* she whispered to the sleeping children. *Yet, even more than that, how I wish Emily were here to see you and kiss you herself!*

She shut the door softly behind her and stood undecided. Should she go into the library and read, with a glass of chilled mint tea, or should she collect her cape and gloves from her room and order her mare to be saddled?

She walked down the long hall to her own door. She had left her long windows open to the evening breeze, and with pleasure she watched it lift the light lace curtains as she walked to her bureau and picked up the printed pamphlet. She had written the address on the back: 111 Wallace Street. Ought she to go? She turned the thin volume over in her hands. *A Voice of Warning,* it was called, written by a man named Pratt who was a minister in The Church of Jesus Christ of Latter-day Saints—the "Mormons." No; it was all nonsense, just as the minister had said it was last week in the kirk. What was she thinking?

She left cape, gloves, and book where they were and went down to the library. Here she met memories of Morag as well. By this fire they had cuddled together on many a dark winter's night, listening to the wet sigh of the wind along the clattering eaves—a sound that, like all wind sounds, sent shivers of delight through both of them. Here Flora had explored the leather-bound books that were old before Morag's time. Here she had dreamed, listening to stories that sounded too much like fairy tales to ever be true: a laird falling in love with a country girl and snatching her away from her young lover's arms, bringing her here, to this place, to this magnificent house, with its gardens and forests and ghosts; soldiers and armies, death and danger, and always the heather cottage somewhere in the middle of it. How life seemed to have changed since then! Flora had been seven years old when her great-grandmother died. For her on that night, that one night, the magic had come true! She had run out to the gardens, Morag's gardens, weeping inconsolably, feeling her young heart must burst with the sorrow that swelled it. And then the sound came. Flute-like music, as airy and light as a fairy tune. She had gulped back her sobs and held her breath, just to listen. She could still remember the sound. If she closed her eyes she could still feel it brush over her, like a caress, like something one could reach out and touch.

She could not stay here tonight. Her spirit was too restless. She had wanted to go to this meeting ever since she had picked up the pamphlet in Charles Hay's store. She must satisfy her curiosity or suffer this annoying unrest. She rang for Nathan Forbes, the estate manager selected for the post by Morag herself when he was a young man of twenty-seven and she well past eighty.

"The old tyrant," Flora's mother had often muttered. "She finds every way she can to extend her influence longer and longer. No chance for others; she snatches every smidgen to herself!" How bitter and whiny her voice had sounded; it made Flora recoil. In her youthful naiveté she had always thought, though she never dared say so, that those *should* have power who can best handle power. Her great-grand-mother's influence, to Flora, was always a gentle, guiding, benign one.

"Oh, I'm sorry, Nathan. Yes, I rang." How long had he been stand-ing there, waiting for her to snap out of her reverie? "Could you saddle Rosie for me?"

He squinted his eyes at her, wanting, she knew, to ask where she was going. But he had been too well bred. "In no time at all," he replied and walked out with that loose, easy rhythm that was charac-teristic of him. Even at fifty-three he still had a lean body and moved like a young man—and had kept, too, that gleam in his eye, which so many Scottish lads had!

It was a pleasant night for a ride. Flora left her hair loose so the summer breeze could blow through it. The ride to Kingussie was not a long one. For a few miles the road skirted the river, with Ravenwood acres extending beyond, then bent in a wide curve and dropped grad-ually. Flora liked the wooded stretch best, where the air turned sud-denly moist and cool, and hidden birds cried out against the intrusion, and all was shadow and green. There was little more of interest until the first humped village cobblestones came into sight. Kingussie. Morag always claimed it hadn't changed in three hundred years; she was probably right. Although not particularly enamored of clusters of houses and humanity, Flora liked the place; she liked the people who lived there, with very few qualifications. As she tied Primrose up before 111 Wallace Street she wondered if she would recognize any of the faces in attendance tonight. A wave of self-conscious hesitation swept over her, but she reminded herself briskly that she was here only as a curious observer. They had best not expect more from her; she would set aright anyone who did.

She was admitted to a modest-sized cottage parlor, clean as a whistle, she noted, and lined with rows of straight kitchen and dining room chairs. The meeting was already in progress, which suited her purposes precisely. She found a seat at the very back and settled against its ungiving wood with a little sigh. Religion was certainly a firebrand men were waving about these days. Unity and unquestion-ing confidence had become things of the past. Hotly held differences were splitting the established church, beloved Presbyterianism, into factions; and everything in life seemed open to question and change.

"How would you define faith in its most unlimited sense? the Prophet Joseph asked. And this is his answer, brothers and sisters: 'Faith, then, is the first great governing principle which has power, dominion, and authority over all things.'"

Flora leaned forward, concentrating her efforts to hear, her interest caught suddenly.

"'By it all things exist, by it they are upheld, by it they are changed, or by it they remain, agreeable to the will of God. Without it there is no power, and without power there could be no creation nor existence!'"

This was more plain than anything Flora had ever heard at the village kirk. It dignified faith beyond mere belief and desire. She liked the feel of the words as they rolled off the speaker's tongue, even though the way he accented them was quite peculiar. She took her first real look at him. He appeared to be about forty—a tall, well-built man with a broad, jutting forehead and a strong chin. And good eyes—the first feature Flora looked for. From this distance they appeared mild and serene, not fired with a fanatic's intemperate zeal. His voice, too, was mildly persuasive, despite the apparent confidence and conviction with which he spoke.

"'God is the only supreme governor and independent being in whom all fullness and perfection dwell; who is omnipotent, omnipresent, and omniscient; without beginning of days or end of life.'"

That principle had always distressed Flora. How could one be expected to fit one's mind around that? Yet these other things Joseph Smith had taught, according to this speaker—she had never heard them before.

"'In him every good gift and every good principle dwell; he is the Father of lights; in him the principle of faith dwells independently, and he is the object in whom the faith of all other rational and accountable beings center for life and salvation.'"

Faith in a God without body, parts, or passions, Flora had always been taught. But a God who embodied all fulness and perfection, who possessed every good gift . . . She was listening now, and during the next hour nothing distracted her attentions from the wonderful ideas she was feasting upon.

She was at the very back, but slipping out was not a possibility. Half a dozen strangers surrounded her, warmly extending their hands, giving names she didn't catch in the hubbub. They seemed genuinely interested in her, pausing to ask questions, but not pressing when they saw her reluctance. Two or three pushed copies of the Book of Mormon upon her, but she shook her head and would not accept one.

"You liked what you heard. Ever so much more is contained in the book."

She knew that voice. Of course! Turning, she looked into the face of the man who had been preaching. "How do you know I liked what I heard?" she demanded.

A brief smile touched his eyes and softened the lines of his face. "I watched you," he said. "I could see it in your eyes as you listened. That book will bring you the same light and peace you just experienced."

She took a step back and shook her head, more vigorously this time. The smile only deepened, warming his features. He drew her hand up between his and patted it, as he might have done with a child. "I understand. I felt much the same way myself once. My wife, bless her heart, saw the truth of things much more quickly than I did. We're not here to push you, my dear."

He moved on, making slow progress across the crowded room, as he paused to speak to so many. The hour was late—goodness! Was it as late as the hands on the clock said?

With steady determination Flora pushed her way to the door. But a glass of tea and a raspberry scone were thrust upon her by a thin wisp of a woman who unintentionally barred the door like a sentry and kept up a stream of lively chatter until Flora, to her own amazement, discovered herself joining in, comparing the colds and fevers Rory and Lilias had suffered last winter with those of the woman's five children, exchanging home remedies, relaxing. Flora didn't know how to socialize; her "station" had always prevented her from learning this skill. She would engage in polite conversation at the kirk on Sundays, to be sure, and help in sickness or times of general disaster or family calamity. But the village people would not be themselves with her the way they were with each other. And the landed gentry? There were not many in this country, and Flora enjoyed their company less than she did that of the common folk. Her brother, Gavin, had seen to that. He had spent a wild, dissipated youth in the company of other young men who had too little to do with their time. To be honest, they had made Flora's stomach turn. She liked solitude and her own ways, much as Morag had. "You're too much like her," Flora's mother used to complain. "How should I be expected to live with the two of you?"

The thin woman took Flora's empty glass and carried it into the kitchen. A natural time to leave. Flora took one last look around. There had been surprisingly few faces she recognized, though most of the strangers appeared to hail from these same parts, judging from their clothing and speech. The man who had delivered the sermon was standing in a corner and was deep in conversation with a younger man; their faces were averted. Flora slipped through the front door unnoticed.

The night had grown windy and cold. A squall appeared to be blowing in from the west. She drew her cape about her, but left the hood down for now. She wished to feel the fingers of the wind in her hair. She set off on Rosie, enjoying the sounds and physical sensations that encased her, not bothering her head about the Mormon meeting at all.

The rain blew over the far hills much sooner than Flora had expected; she would be wet to the skin before she got home. Her hood was snug about her cheeks and chin now, and she bent over her horse's neck, guiding her carefully. Yet neither one saw the ragged hole, camouflaged as part of a long, muddy puddle. Primrose lost her footing and stumbled, going nearly down to her knees before righting herself. It was too sudden: Flora landed with a hard whack on the ground, one leg twisted beneath her. She cried out at the shock of hot pain that tremored up her leg. Soaked and shivering, she crawled to the edge of the road and rested in the cushion of slick, matted grass. Her leg was throbbing. She touched it gingerly and winced. But that appeared to be the only place she was injured.

Rosie stood over her with a forlorn expression. "Yes, we're in a regular fix, you and I," she muttered up at the animal. The horse seemed uninjured. If Flora could only stand and somehow manage to mount her . . .

But the effort to do so made her sink, weak and trembling, to the ground again. She needed a tree, or even a stump, to support her. She peered through the screen of darkness and rain and with great distaste dragged herself over the mud and mulched leaves to a young rowan as slimy and soaked as herself but whose girth was narrow enough that she could wrap her arms entirely around it. By slow stages she pulled herself upright, then stood on one foot, trembling and dizzy, and stared out into the dripping forest. She knew well that she needed help of some kind. Rosie was a high-strung, skittish thing, and Flora could see no log or stump she might use to help her mount.

You might well spend the night here, alone with the storm and the shad-

ows, a voice whispered from some place inside herself. And Flora knew it was true. Few people used this road, fewer still at this hour. And the storm would obscure her and render her efforts to communicate her presence pitiful and futile. She closed her eyes. She liked the sound the rain made as it struck the moist green leaves. She liked the sharp, earthy smells.

With her eyes closed still she began to pray, and as she did so the Mormon speaker's face came into her mind, and the way he had prayed: "Heavenly Father, we know that thou lovest thy children. We are grateful for the truths which teach us of thee and thy ways." What else had he said? Something about truth giving us joy and freedom, so that we could become like God. The words had sounded strange and brash. But they had felt warm and familiar sinking into her heart.

Please help me, she prayed. *Please help someone to find me, someone good and trustworthy.* Would highwaymen harry the roads in such weather? she wondered, remembering, against her will, stories that made her shudder. *Send someone,* she implored, *and help me to know I can trust him, some sign*—But wasn't it wrong to pray for signs? Flora had not prayed much in her life—only the formal prayers which were required, of course, and there were times when her father gathered his small, reticent family in prayer. But those, too, were special occasions, the sacred Christian holidays which all good Presbyterian families observed. And in seasons of famine or flood the congregation joined with the minister in importuning heaven for aid. Nothing wholly personal; nothing at all like this.

"I learned to pray at a young age." Flora smiled at the memory of the words, so often spoken to her, and the look on her great-grandmother's face—one of serene determination, if such a thing could be. But at times when Morag said those words her eyes would be sad, troubled with the memories of old pains which still had power to wound, or at least subdue her.

"I'm so cold," Flora said out loud. Perhaps she ought to move back, closer to the edge of the road again. Who would spy her huddled among the trees? But here at least there was a form of shelter. She shrank from full exposure to the wild, slashing rain.

How long had it been since she fell? Though it felt like hours, it was probably only a matter of minutes. A whole night to be spent this way? She moaned aloud at the prospect. *Send someone I can trust, send someone good to help me!*

A rumble of thunder struck her ears and shook the aspens. No, it wasn't thunder, but the wheels of a carriage, and horses! Startled, Rosie whinnied and reared, striking out at the unseen threat. Flora took a careening step forward, then fell to her knees. Like a black boulder the carriage rolled toward them. So near . . . so near! Flora shut her eyes tight, not willing to watch it swing past and leave her. So she gasped when she opened them to see a face close above hers—a young, anxious face.

"Thank heaven your horse reared and I found you." He gathered her into his arms and lifted her as easily, and gently, as he might have lifted a small sleeping child. "You are hurt?"

"My leg," she explained, "I can't step on it."

Someone was standing beside the carriage and holding the door open. Her rescuer lowered her carefully inside. Then he was there beside her, tucking a soft blanket around her, wiping the mud from her face. "Flora, you poor dear! What a wretched thing to happen to a lady! Do you live near here?"

She nodded. "A few miles up the road."

His eyes widened. "That big house at the top of the hill? I noticed it when I passed this morning." He fumbled in his pocket. "Here, Flora, can you manage to drink a little?" He held a slim cask to her lips. She shook her head again.

"I don't like whiskey, it makes me light-headed." She saw that he wanted to laugh at her, but he wasn't sure that he should. It was too dark to tell his features clearly, but he had a wonderful voice—the way he had said, "Flora, can you manage to drink a little?"

She gasped and reached out for him. He turned concerned eyes to her. "How did you know my name?" she exclaimed.

"Your name?"

"Yes, my name. You called me by name, but I didn't tell you my name. I never spoke it."

His expression grew troubled. "Flora. I called you Flora. Is that your name?"

She nodded.

"Somehow I knew that it was."

He leaned out and gave instructions for his driver to tie Rosie behind the carriage and drive slowly on to the great house which topped the far rise. As the carriage shuddered into movement he leaned back against the cushion and turned to face her.

"You were at the meeting tonight." It was not a question, and he continued. "I tried to learn who you were. But no one had met you.

Even Elder Ramsey, who talked with you, failed to ask your name. I was disappointed to leave without learning it." His voice trailed off, low and thoughtful. Should she tell him that her prayers had brought him here? No, heavens no!

"There is some reason, some definite reason." He was studying her face so intently that she felt flustered and dropped her own eyes.

"You're still shivering," he said suddenly. "Is your leg hurting awfully?"

It was, but she shook her head at him. He pushed her tangled hair back from her forehead. "You don't have to put on a brave face for me. I'm here to help you."

How could a voice be both vibrant and tender, the way his voice was? It sent a warm tremor through her entire being. She leaned back against the cushion and told him what had happened.

"I think I should go for a doctor," he said.

"It is very late. I can send Nathan first thing in the morning."

He knit his forehead, and one bushy eyebrow arched upward. "Who is Nathan?" he asked.

"Our factor."

"He manages your father's estate?"

"Yes." She held back a somewhat embarrassed smile. Would he run off, be frightened away if she told him Ravenwood belonged solely to her? No father, no brother, no husband had claim on it.

They were no longer moving. He pushed the door open and stuck his head out. "We're here."

In no time at all he had his driver leading Rosie to the stables, and he had taken the key she gave him and unlatched the door. To her amazement a light in the library was burning. She had him carry her there. Nathan Forbes was dozing in her grandfather's big leather chair, waiting. His face brightened with relief when he saw her.

"You had trouble! You met with an accident on the road; well I knew it—I should not have let you be out so late, miss, alone!" He bent over her, fidgeting like an old wife. She waved him away from her. "Stop, both of you!" she pleaded. "I shall be fine."

When she insisted that no doctor be called, Nathan insisted that at least he wake Izzy to wash Flora and put her to bed. When he scurried off to do so, she looked at her benefactor. "You have not told me *your* name."

"Colin Fraser. I drove over from Paisley, and I am most happy that my brother lent me his carriage and insisted I come."

Flora felt not the least bit tired. She was curious, and anxious to talk. "Have you been to other Mormon meetings?"

"A few, yes."

"Are they always the same?"

"Pretty much. They've got strange doctrine, but they're not the screaming, wild-eyed devils some people make them out to be. I believe my brother just might join with them, though he hasn't said so as yet."

"What a frightening prospect!"

She murmured the words reflectively, and he responded in the same spirit. "Commitment on any level is frightening, and commitment to anything this demanding, this out of the ordinary . . ."

"Are their tenets demanding?"

"I'd say. Did you pick up a copy of the Book of Mormon at the meeting?"

"No, I didn't."

"Well, here, take mine." He drew it from the large pocket of his great coat. "My brother has another, and I can always get more copies."

He held it out to her. She placed her hands on it gingerly, feeling a powerful resistance within her. "Now, you must not only take it, you must read it, so that next time I come we can have a proper discussion."

"Next time? I think you and your man had best spend the night."

"No, no." He was adamant. "My brother would miss me and worry. He's used to my hours. Even if I drag in late, at least I'll be there in the morning. Otherwise he'd fret himself to death. We'll be fine on the road; we're used to it, Samuel and I."

Nathan and Izzy entered, and Colin Fraser made his farewells and was gone amid the confusion, without what Flora considered a valid good-bye. Nor did he explain his strange comment: "So that next time I come." He must have spoken the words out of politeness only— lightly spoken, lightly forgotten. What difference should that make to her? Why should it make her feel cross and disappointed? Perhaps it was only the accident and the pain in her leg. So she told herself as Nathan carried her up the broad stairs to her room. But something within her knew better, and some voice inside kept whispering: *He knew your name. How is it that he was brought to your rescue? How is it that he called you by name?*

16

$\mathcal{D}$r. Fletcher came in the morning. He assured Flora she had suffered an extremely bad sprain. He bound her foot tightly and told her, with a no-nonsense tone, that she must stay off it for several days. He would check back in a week's time, sooner if she felt she had need of him. Flora could remember being confined only once—with a childhood disease. But Morag had entertained her and made the days pass splendidly. Now her mother fussed about in her annoying, distracted way, and Rory and Lilias whined for her, distressed by the upset of their accustomed schedule. They were too young to be of much help. Their noises and constant running backward and forward across the room made her head ache, until at last she sent them away.

"I was right," her mother complained. "If you had engaged a proper nurse for them, as I once pleaded with you to do, there would be someone to care for them now. Izzy can't be expected to handle everything."

Flora was genuinely disgusted. "Izzy doesn't 'handle everything.' She has Cook and the two girls who do most of her housework. Besides," she added, unable to help herself, "you could care for the children yourself. You might find you enjoy it."

Her mother wrinkled her nose in distaste, so that Flora burst out, "Precisely. Look at yourself! But for Grandmother, I would have been raised by a nursemaid. You know I wanted Emily's children to be raised by a mother."

Rowena Douglas sniffled and her Irish-blue eyes filled with tears. "My poor little Emily. Dead these two years and cold in her grave. Remember her voice when she laughed, Flora? Remember how she read poetry to you, or sang to you, here in this very room summer nights?"

Flora nodded grimly, while her mother dabbed at her red eyes. *Why does remembering bring out an anger in me?* she wondered, then realized that it wasn't the remembering itself but her mother's manner of remembering that sat ill with her. By herself Flora could wallow in grief and nostalgia for hours on end. Besides, it was not the loss of Emily they had been discussing, but the upbringing and happiness of the two precious children she'd left behind. *How can Mother appear to care so much, and in actuality keep her own self aloof?* Flora had wondered the same thing, really, since she herself was a child. *You could love Emily's children in lieu of Emily herself,* she wanted to say. But she had said it before. It accomplished no good, brought no communication whatsoever. *We've never been compatible,* she concluded sadly, *and it's true that Grandmother's influence tended to aggravate that. But without Grandmother, what a dearth my life would have been!*

During the first day of confinement Flora chafed against each new restriction, each altered condition imposed upon her, and the altered household chafed, too. By the third day everyone was making adjustments. But the inaction drove Flora wild. Her two options were sewing and reading, and she was not much of a one for sewing. Late on the third afternoon she picked up the Book of Mormon which Colin Fraser had handed her. Perhaps she would read for a while. Perhaps he might return, and she would not wish to disappoint him.

She finished the book on the fifth day. She had grown very quiet. All of a sudden she had much on her mind, many things to question, consider, mull over carefully. There had been things in the book which she did not understand. But there had been too much that she did, too much that pierced the inadequate shell of protection around her heart, and she was astonished at the light which filled her whole soul at such moments. If only those moments would last!

The evening of the fourth day after her fall her mother had come into the library and noticed what book she was reading.

"I'll have none of that here," she bristled. "Flora, you ought to know better. The Mormons are a despised sect. They believe in strange, horrible things."

Flora couldn't help laughing. "Heavens no, Mother, don't fret yourself. There is much of interest in here."

"Much to cause our neighbors to laugh at us and point the finger of scorn, daughter."

"There's more to life than fretting about the opinion of one's neighbors, Mother." Flora tried to say the words gently. How she longed for an answering light of comprehension to gleam in those placid blue eyes that gazed back at her! *Draw up a chair,* she longed to say. *See what you think of this.*

"'Tis dangerous nonsense, Flora. I want none of it." *Her usual exaggerated retort,* Flora thought, as her mother bustled out of the room. The long library windows stood open. Flora could smell the summer grass with a faint mingling of blossoms. She closed her eyes, trying to lose herself in the peace of it. But a terrible loneliness encased her, shutting out all peace and filling her with an aching longing which sent tears to her eyes.

The doctor came and went again. Flora was much improved. "Youth," he said, smiling, "heals quickly." She hobbled about with the aid of her grandfather's cane. She sat in the garden shade and let Rory and Lilias play at her feet, her nerves no longer jangled by their shrill, bubbling voices. Yet, she was thinking past them, for the first time in over two years.

It was more than duty, surely, which bade me wrap my life round theirs, she reasoned with herself. *Love. Love only.* No, there had also been need, her own need to feel a purpose in living, a calling beyond mere day-to-day existence. Children are easy to immerse oneself in, especially children this small. From the beginning she had felt no sense of confinement or frustration in taking care of them, only the sweetest joy and fulfillment. It had disturbed her a little, to be truthful, when Emily married before she did. But Flora was herself only twenty-three when the first child was born. Now both Emily and her handsome young husband were dead, killed in a runaway coach on the highroad to London, and there were two bairns left behind. And Flora was suddenly twenty-seven, and that frightened her. Women in this family followed an obvious pattern of marrying young, very young. She was a maid still at twenty-seven, and she was suddenly beginning to feel time as a living thing, a powerful force pushing her on, snatching her days from her and dangling a dark, silent image of loneliness before her reluctant gaze.

When the children went in for their nap Flora lingered in the garden, Morag's garden, though Flora had often heard her great-grandmother say, "I could never maintain it quite as splendid as I found it. Anne Lockhart created this garden, you know. She created Ravenwood, the soul of the place as it is, the way you and I feel it today." Nevertheless, Flora felt herself even more wanting in the graces and skills that were needed. She had old Fergus, a true gardener, despite age and stiff arthritic fingers. His patient skills kept the garden thriving. Flora spent more and more of her time with the children, and found she came here only to enjoy—to partake, not impart.

But today she felt no uneasy guilt for that. With the scent of lavender in her nostrils she leaned back and closed her eyes, feeling the warmth of the sun seep through her skin to warm the very insides of her.

"A lady of leisure we have here. Dare I interrupt such a beautiful reverie?" The words were spoken lightly, but with no hint at mockery. It was a voice she had heard before, a voice that sent shivers along her warm skin.

When she opened her eyes his face was nearly as close to hers as it had been that night. She gasped and put her hand to her throat, nervously fingering the lace there.

"I should not have come unannounced," he apologized. But his candid, dancing eyes belied his words, and suddenly he laughed and shook his head at his own foolishness. "Please don't be flustered or, worse, angry with me. To be truthful, I had not the courage to go about the thing properly."

"And why, sir, is that?"

"For fear I would be denied, forbidden to see you. I had to avoid that possibility at all costs."

She laughed with him, to cover the astonishment his words caused, and the sincerity behind them, too obvious to ignore.

"This is an enchanting place," Colin Fraser said, pulling a chair close. "Despite the elegance, there is a true, quiet beauty here."

Despite the elegance. "How do you make your living, Colin," she asked, "that you come calling midday, at your leisure?"

He had thick, raven black hair, which he wore long, and eyes of a startling blue, which danced back at her now. "Nothing so grand," he replied, glancing about him, "but respectable and solid, I can assure you. My father owns a mill in Paisley, and I run it for him."

"My brother runs a mill there." She smiled, a bit ruefully. "It belongs to his father-in-law, though he's already purchased a large share in it."

"I would know him, surely."

Flora hesitated briefly. "Gavin Douglas of Carmichael and Son."

Colin sat silent a moment, one eyebrow arched thoughtfully.

"You do know him. You may be candid."

"I know of him, even met him a time or two. Pompous little thing, isn't he?"

"Very. Always was, and marrying didn't help any."

"*Has* Carmichael a son?"

"He did. But the boy died of typhus when still a lad. That's how Gavin has wormed his way in so deeply. Now all his hopes center on Agatha, and knowing that, Gavin is bleeding the old man dry, I'm afraid."

Colin nodded. "Well, well. Too bad," he said thoughtfully. "Let us talk now of pleasant things—of the book you've been reading."

What a strange one he was! "How do you know I've been reading it? And, if you've read it yourself, you know it's far from pleasant. It has been most disturbing to me."

"Flora, Flora, you are so intense about everything! The book is filled with beauty and wonder, and you know it. Jesus Christ dealing with people on the American continent!"

"Of course an American prophet would say that."

Colin laughed again. "In my opinion, there's no such thing as an American anything, not yet, anyway; the country's too new. Joseph Smith's ancestors came from England and Scotland—did you know that?"

"No."

"Men like Nephi and Captain Moroni, Jesus praying for the little children and blessing them, the sermons of King Mosiah—no man made up those things in his head, no unschooled farm boy scarcely past twenty. You felt it, Flora." He had found her hand and was clasping it tightly between his. "Tell me, please. Tell me what's in your heart."

Uncomfortably the picture of herself on that black night in the woods flashed before her eyes, and the words of her prayer ran through her head: *Please send someone good to help me, someone I can trust.*

The blue eyes were watching her. She drew a deep breath and began to speak, plainly and openly, holding nothing back.

They talked all afternoon. Izzy brought tea and they drank it, hardly stopping for breath. Flora came not only to know Colin Fraser, but to know herself, as her efforts to communicate revealed things she had always kept safely hidden before. The slanting summer light, mellow and golden, seemed to reflect the light that had suddenly flared into life within her. Like a strength Flora felt it; like a beauty she saw it reflected back in Colin's bright eyes.

The final interruption came when, with the lengthening shadows, Izzy insisted that Flora move inside, at least to the fainting couch in the library where she could stretch out and lie back. Flora pressed Colin to take the evening meal with them before riding the long hours home.

"'Tis already arranged, miss," Izzy said stolidly. "Cook's planned double portions for him, and I've set an extra place at table."

Flora was curious as to how her mother would receive the stranger. But her mother was easy to charm, and Colin was a fair one for charming, so they got on very well. Flora enjoyed watching him. He possessed such an uncommon mingling of gentleness and vivacity. Everything in life was of interest to him. He observed things with meticulous attention to detail, yet his conversation was not tedious, but lively and colored with the wonder and enthusiasm with which he viewed life. And he was a good listener; his curiosity, if nothing else, made him so. Like a new piece of furniture that accentuates the shabbiness of the old and worn fare, his presence seemed to accentuate the shabby, sluggish nature of Flora's days. Too soon the meal ended, too soon she was ensconced on the couch, an invalid again, and he was preparing to leave. Her mother hovered, and it appeared he might depart in this vacuum, when Izzy poked in her head and asked, "Dare I bring down the little ones?"

Then there was enchantment indeed. Colin had a way with children. He sat cross-legged on the floor between them, examining their toys with serious and tender regard, answering their questions, telling stories that sent them into high, breathless peals of laughter or held them in a net of suspense and silence. Rory clung to his hand and Flora thought, with a twinge of pain, *He needs a man in his life, poor little lad.* Only promises, then threats, accompanied by tears, enticed the children away from Colin. *He has charmed the entire household,* Flora realized uneasily. *Is our hunger and loneliness so pathetically obvious to him?*

In the sudden silence of the children's departure—they being herded out by both her mother and Izzy—Colin turned to Flora with a dark, thoughtful expression. "They are beautiful children," he said. "You did not tell me about them."

"They are my sister's children." She sighed, not noticing the sudden relaxing of his features. "She was very young when she died. She and her husband were both killed in an accident . . ." An unbidden memory came to her—of Emily's pale, childlike features as she lay like a frail fairy princess in her casket.

Colin had placed his hand over hers; how warm and firm it felt! "And you took her children and cared for them."

"I wished them to be raised by a mother, by someone who loved them."

"Oh, one can tell they have been, tenderly loved and cared for." His words sent a singular joy pulsing through her. "So you've had no need to marry, with these bairns to draw out your affections."

"The women in the Douglas line marry young. I had every intention of doing so, and I had offers aplenty, but I wanted what my grandmother had, the kind of love that could make her eyes shine when she was nearly ninety. Not a marriage like my parents had, and so many others I'd seen."

She tugged her hand away, horrified when she realized what she had said to him. Growing hot with embarrassment she dropped her eyes, avoiding his gaze.

"Such true mingling of a man's spirit and a woman's spirit is indeed rare, Flora Douglas." He whispered the words, and she could feel his breath warm on her hair. "I am glad you did not settle for less." He pressed his lips to her hair; then with a soft, burning tingling she felt their sweet touch on her cheek. She trembled, aching with his tenderness, longing for more, longing for this feeling to never leave her, but he drew suddenly back. With an annoying bustle and rustle of skirts her mother entered the room.

And, as before, in the confusion, the polite, impersonal vacuum, he left her—walked away as he had the first time, with no plans laid, no promises, nothing to extend into the future. He took the fair moment with him. And what future could her dull days retain without his spirit breathing life and hope through them?

She buried her face in the cushion that yet held the odor of her great-grandmother's perfume and her soft, fragrant skin. And she wept, pretending for a moment that Morag's kind arms encircled her still, that the soothing voice sang the old lullaby to her, easing her fears and her pain.

17

$\mathcal{T}$he letter arrived by messenger. Izzy brought it into the children's nursery, where Rory was riding his rocking horse and Lilias was dressing her dolls. Puzzled, Flora tore open the seal. The paper was dated August 17, the day before yesterday. It had been nearly three weeks since she had seen Colin Fraser. Now he was inviting her, summoning her really, to a Latter-day Saint conference to be held in Paisley the following week. He would send his brother's carriage for her, and, unless she preferred staying with her own brother, she was welcome to stay with Kenneth and his wife. His family were all anxious to meet her. He signed his name with a firm flourish and added as a postscript: "Come prepared for a long, pleasurable visit. You deserve one."

She stood staring at the letter, smiling gently to herself. Even his written words seemed to convey the vibrant life of his spirit. Ought she to go? She smoothed the paper with her fingers. He had touched this. He had written the words to her only. What thoughts had been in his mind, what images or memories of her? She shook her head and laughed at herself. Vain, girlish imaginings, inappropriate for a mature woman approaching thirty!

She bent and peered into the small oval mirror atop Lilias's dressing table. Thick brown hair, escaping in long curling tendrils, encircled a face "framed for beauty," as her mother put it. Indeed, she had her mother's Irish blue eyes and white skin. But the firm line of her chin, the long elegant nose came from Morag Macpherson undoubtedly. Her graceful neck, which showed gold and jewels off to advantage, and her small, finely shaped hands came from Anne—Morag used to hold Flora's hands up and say, "These hands come from Annie Lockhart, and so does your will, your gentle, unbendable determination." They were pretty words, even to a child who did not understand them. Perhaps Morag had been merely wishing such things. Flora felt no extraordinary force of personality within herself, nothing bright and unusual. She had lived a common life, really, filled with little to challenge or try her.

Ought she really to go? *Of course!* she told herself firmly. *Else I will display no determination at all and must count myself willy-nilly for the rest of my life.*

Rory toddled over and put his head in her lap. Absently she stroked the soft down of his hair. She realized with a shock that she had never been separated from the children for more than a long day; there had never been any need. Now, for the first time—

"Mither, rock me to sleep," the child asked, his voice already mumbled and drowsy.

"You—a great lad of four!" she teased, pulling him onto her lap, hugging his body warm against hers. *Mother.* What word in any language sounded lovelier, held more tenderness in its syllables? She still felt guilty from time to time for claiming the title. But she *was* the only mother they knew. And they ought to feel secure with her, knowing she truly belonged to them.

The words came to her of their own accord: *List to the curlew cryin', faint are the echoes dyin'* . . . The echoes of a voice in her head saying, *One can tell they have been tenderly loved.* The salve of kindness to her lonely heart. Why could she not dislodge that tender voice from her mind? Why had desire for him spoiled everything else for her, and revealed the narrow dimensions of her narrow existence, making her hunger for the rich, all-embracing relish of life that was his?

Flora awoke to sounds and smells that were entirely new to her. There was nothing of birdsong and silence here. Colin's brother, Kenneth, she discovered, was an older edition of Colin, cut out of much the same cloth. And his young wife, Janet, though a shy little thing, was terribly solicitous and kind, and would talk if drawn out a bit. Flora had liked them both from the start, when Kenneth's carriage pulled up to his own door and he and Janet were waiting to greet her, assuming she would wish to stay with them. No one had mentioned her brother at all. She had been washed and fed and rested from her journey and all settled in before Colin had arrived from the mill, cleaned and polished himself, and ready to show her the town.

Paisley had been little more than a village for many years, but it was congested now, bursting its seams with the influx of hundreds of Highlanders and Irishmen come to work in the city, most out of necessity, many against their own will. There was a flavor of diversity here and the constant stirring of different kinds of people, each enriching the landscape in some way of his own. Flora liked it. She liked the crowded restaurant where they ate delicious pastries and she tried Welsh rarebit for the first time. In their conversation Flora learned that Kenneth ran a mill of his own in nearby Kilbarchan, a mill that wove clan tartans.

"Fifty looms I have. Next year a hundred," he boasted. Janet smiled quietly, enjoying her husband's enthusiasm. Flora enjoyed it, too, enjoyed the easy comradeship that existed among them. Religion was not broached that night. Only mills and workers and the progress that industry promised. New, young dreams. Flora had never before had a part in them. But she did not feel like an outsider here. Their dreams reached out to embrace her, and she did not feel herself a stranger in any sense.

Late, very late, she had walked the dark streets with Colin, at ease with him after the familiarity of the evening. "Do you wish to be a big, successful businessman, then, Colin?" she asked him. "With hundreds of men answerable to you and hundreds of families dependent upon your good will?"

He looked at her and shuddered. "You paint it a horrid prospect, Flora! Better me than some others. You might look at it that way. I have ideas . . ." His voice grew a bit dreamy and his eyes became soft. "Kenneth and I have our eye on Robert Owen over New Lanark way, who does things for his workers no one else would even dream of. We're putting our heads together to see what we can manage ourselves."

"I'm not sure what you're talking about."

"Well, most of the conditions in the mills are disgraceful. People like your brother, I fear, think only of profit and look upon the people who work for them in much the same way as they regard their machines."

Flora nodded grimly. "I know. That's why I do not wish to see him. I have visited him one time only, shortly after he married, and for me that was enough and to spare! I don't know how Agatha puts up with him." She sighed. "His cruel ways distress me. He talks of nothing but money and profit, and the things money can buy."

"Hush, now! I've distressed you, when I did not mean to." Colin drew up her hand and pressed his lips against it. "Let us take leave of men and their affairs. The night is too lovely, and I soil the sweet moments with such talk." His eyes swam with tenderness. "Have we not some unfinished business, lass, you and I?"

He drew her into his arms and covered her mouth with his own. His lips were warm; she could feel them entreating her, claiming her. The last thing she saw before she closed her eyes and touched his smooth hair with her hand was a cluster of thin black chimneys etched against the gray sky, where never a bird nor a leafy tree ventured. But here in this rank, sooty air she tasted a deep, sweet wonder that Morag's gardens, for all their beauty, had never shown her.

LATTER-DAY SAINTS
The Paisley Branch of this Society
now meet for Public Worship in
MR. MACARTHUR'S GRAND HALL

The poster before Flora's eyes was large, with bold lettering; it listed the times of meetings each Sabbath, and other information as well. "The public are respectfully invited to attend," it read at the bottom. But the meeting today, Colin reminded her, was a conference, drawing in all the small congregations of members, which they called "branches," in the area.

"Paisley was the first branch organized," he told her, "May eighth of last year. Just look how phenomenally they've grown!"

It was phenomenal—frightening, really. There were three or four hundred people at least crammed into the large hall. Flora had to admit that they all seemed polite and well mannered, and friendly. Despite the obviously humble, or even shabby, appearance of many, their faces betrayed their emotions: the peace which could not be mistaken, and eager eyes, lighting with warmth upon recognizing a fellow.

"There is no drunkenness among these people," Colin whispered, as they found places to sit. "Temperance in all things, subduing the flesh so that the spirit might prosper."

"How do you know so much?"

"I told you, Kenneth is serious about this. 'Tis all he talks of."

The meeting opened with prayer followed by a hymn, one Flora was familiar with, so she sang along.

> Praise ye the Lord! My heart shall join
> In work so pleasant, so divine,
> Now, while the flesh is my abode,
> And when my soul ascends to God.

Flora felt her face grow warm, unable to prevent thoughts of the flesh, thoughts which filled her mind for the first time, thoughts which were tempting and sweet.

Happy the man whose hopes rely
On Israel's God! He made the sky
And earth and seas with all their train,
And none shall find his promise vain.

It was obvious to Flora that these people about her trusted in Israel's God. She trusted in little, she feared. At Emily's death she had been devastated, and when her father died shortly after, leaving her alone with two helpless children, and a distraught, helpless mother—oh, she had yearned then for comfort and spiritual strength! And, actually, had she not felt lost and empty since that time? She knew what soul-hunger was, the aching needs of the spirit.

A man rose to speak. It was Alexander Wright, one of the first two missionaries to Scotland, a native Scot returning from Canada, a Banffshire man. He wore a long, drooping red mustache, and a full beard that was more gray than brown, and he had the broad, jutting forehead of the Scotsman, and the deep-set twinkling eyes. Flora liked him at once, and when he spoke of the Prophet Joseph, as he called him, and the things he had suffered to bring forth the truth, Flora felt a sudden, astounding conviction: *That man is a prophet of God. He is all he claims to be.*

She dropped her eyes, lest someone read her thoughts in her face. She could not question the validity or strength of the conviction that sat like a quiet benediction upon her heart. She noticed nothing else. The commotion drew near before she lifted her head, startled. Colin reached for her hand.

"Factory bosses," he whispered, leaning close to her. "Come to frighten the people."

One walked but two rows away from them, carrying a large stick in his hand. "'Twill go poorly for you, MacGregor, that your face has been seen here." His voice was a growl, but the man he was addressing ignored him. "Wallace—Buchanan!" He began calling out names.

"How dare he?" Flora hissed, clutching Colin's hand until he tugged to release it. "Flora!"

But suddenly she went stiff and cold, so still and stiff that he bent over her. "Heaven help me, Colin, 'tis my brother Gavin—right there!"

They sat far enough back in the hall that the commotion the men caused was as yet nothing more than a rude, annoying disturbance. But how far would the intruders go? *Please turn, please walk in a different direction,* Flora willed her brother, *then I can slip out of my seat. And run away from him?*

She drew a deep breath and sat up straighter. "Let him see me," she whispered to Colin. "I am not one of his poor, mistreated workers. I have nothing to fear from him."

Gavin did see her. As though sensing her presence, he turned slowly all the way round. His eyes fixed on her; he shook his head to dislodge the dread image. She nodded her head ever so slightly, with perfect courtesy, toward him, then turned her eyes on the speaker, using all her energies not to weaken and glance to see his reaction. But Colin watched him covertly. Gavin raised the stick that he grasped and shook it at her. Colin was glad Flora had not seen her brother's eyes, seen the terrible hatred that lashed out with more bruising force than if he had struck with his stick.

The disturbance the men made became quite nasty and loud before a constable appeared with his uniform and no-nonsense air, and the hecklers left quietly enough.

"They've accomplished what they came for—makes little difference at this point." Colin's voice was sad, but his words were clipped and short, with an angry edge to them. *Will he fight back if things get bad enough?* Flora wondered. *Of such men as Colin, with their idealism and fervor, are martyrs made.* The thought ran like a cold current through her. The speaker's voice, seeming from a great distance now, droned on. *What am I doing here?* She thought miserably. *I don't belong here. I'm not like these people, I do not seek what they seek.*

But just then Colin reached for her hand and smiled at her with his eyes—deep, kind eyes, eyes one could get lost in. *Send someone to help me, someone I can trust, someone kind . . .* She would never have met this man, never have known he existed, save for these people who called themselves Latter-day Saints. Where was this leading her? Why had it happened? What was she to do?

The closing song began. She had never before heard it, but the strong, simple melody carried a dignity that thrilled her. She sat still, straining to make out the words.

> The visions and blessings of old are returning,
> And angels are coming to visit the earth.

We'll sing and we'll shout with the armies of heaven,
Hosanna, hosanna to God and the Lamb!
Let glory to them in the highest be given,
Henceforth and forever, Amen and amen!

Perhaps Flora did not understand all the meaning of what the words said. That made no difference, not now. *"The Spirit of God like a fire is burning!"* She felt it with too much force to deny it. And the feeling was joy, joy and strength surging through her, and she recognized it as the same feeling she had experienced from time to time while reading the Book of Mormon. She recognized it as the same feeling that had engulfed her that dark, stormy night when a gentle stranger lifted her in his arms and called her by name. She sat bathed in the feeling, exulting in it long after the music had ceased, so that Colin had to shake her a little.

"Flora, 'tis time to leave. And I do believe we ought to be among the first out of the building, for caution's sake."

She rose with him, she went through certain motions and responses, but her heart was still caught up with sensations that did not belong to this world, and she felt as though a soft covering of love encircled her, protecting her from all that was evil, crass, or unseemly. And so, in her own sphere of light and beauty, she walked by Colin's side.

Following the meeting Colin took Flora to his father's home, where Colin still lived, in a suite of rooms of his own. She had met the old gentleman and his wife only briefly, but they welcomed her most kindly now. Colin had work he must do at the mill, but he would return before supper. She sat in the parlor with both of them. Jean, Colin's mother, was smooth faced and rosy cheeked and seemed to sparkle with an exuberance one expected to see in a girl, not a mature woman past fifty. But, somehow, she got away with it. Today she took up her sewing and a bright thread of chatter that carried everyone with it, like a runaway horse. Flora was merely listening, and nodding from time to time, wondering idly how long this could last, when Ewen Fraser coughed deep in his throat, knocked the ashes from his pipe, and said simply, "You had some trouble, I understand, at the Mormon meeting."

Flora looked up. Jean Fraser had stopped, only her knitting needles clicking as fast as her tongue had been. Ewen looked older than his wife, with his snow white beard and long mustache. But his eyes held that same sparkle.

"Yes, sir, I'm afraid that we did."

"'Tis to be expected. Is it not always the way with something new, something that threatens?" He combed his long mustache thoughtfully with the stem of his pipe, drawing it through the silken hairs time after time. "Most of those who oppose the Mormons oppose the reforms some of the rest of us wish to push through. Filth and ignorance serve their purposes, not enlightened, thinking men and women."

Flora liked this man. Though his words made her shiver, she liked how he spoke, how he thought. The sharp knock on the door startled all of them. Ewen looked up with calm, thoughtful eyes. When his butler entered the hall, the old man arose with easy agility. "I believe I ought to see to this, Sandy."

He crossed the room without haste, though the persistent banging had grown louder. The voice Flora heard as the door opened astonished her, took her completely by surprise. She sank back against the cushions, feeling her heartbeat increase to a painful pace in her breast.

"I believe my sister is a guest in your home, sir, and I apologize for any embarrassment or concern she may have caused you. My carriage stands ready."

Jean Fraser leaned close and whispered, with the air of a mischievous conspirator, "Sit up straight and lively, my dear. You don't wish your brother to see you that way, and Ewen may very well bring him right in."

Flora almost giggled. That was precisely what she needed. Gavin *was* inside, standing on the threshold, legs spread in a stubborn pose. He took a few heavy strides forward until his glaring eyes found her.

"Flora, by heaven's name," he roared, "what has come over you?"

She blinked back at him and smiled blandly, trying to arrange her face the way Jean Fraser did.

"You come to Paisley without so much as a word to me, and then proceed to conduct yourself as an unthinking idiot! I must find my own sister in the midst of fanatics and inciters, disgracing *my* reputation, disgracing—"

Ewen stepped out from behind him, coughing gently to draw his attention. "That will do, young man," he said firmly. "You are a guest in my house. You have come to ask your sister a question."

"I have come to take her home! Where she belongs!"

"Your sister is here, as I understand, sir, of her own free will. She is an adult, a landed woman, and may therefore conduct her affairs as she chooses."

Flora was relaxing. She sensed at once that Ewen Fraser was not merely putting on a show of courtesy and control to impress his over-emotional guest. This was the man himself, the sincere expression of what resided within him.

"Miss Douglas, do you desire to accompany your brother home at this time?"

"I do not, sir. I have unfinished business in this place, and—"

"Flora, I am warning you! 'Tis well and good to wax belligerent with this stubborn old man to protect you. You must stop this non-sense and do as I say."

Ewen placed his hand on the younger man's arm, but Gavin shook him off like a furious terrier. "You will not get away with this! There are ways I can hurt you."

"Enough, young man! Your rudeness will no longer be endured here." More quickly than the eye moves Ewen grabbed Gavin's arm and twisted it securely behind his back. Gavin swore and struggled, and swore again, but by this time he had been dragged to the door. With one hard shove Ewen released his arm and propelled him out-side the house.

"Do not come back until you've learned some manners, young man. Until you do, you are not welcome here!"

He wiped his hands back and forth a few times, shut the door, and returned, settling into his accustomed seat and reaching for his cold pipe. He pulled it absently through the curved hairs of his mustache. "Did I hear you say we are having salmon for dinner, Jeannie?"

"That's right, dear. Freshly caught. And I instructed Cook to pre-pare it with your favorite sauce."

"Excellent!" He tapped tobacco into the bowl of his pipe. "Miss Douglas, you must dine with us. No one can bring out the flavor in fish the way our Millie does."

"And Colin would be so pleased." Jean beamed gently on both of them.

Flora smiled back, astonished. That was the end of it, apparently, the unpleasant affair. They were too gracious, too preoccupied with living to prolong distress, and worry over it like an old bone; there was no pettiness here. She was beginning to see what it was about Colin that was so gentle, so rare and delightful, so blissfully safe.

18

It was the first time Flora had ever arrived at Ravenwood with a sense of reluctance. But as the carriage slowed and pulled into the long drive she knew too well what it marked—days of loneliness stretching before her. Here was all she held dear: Morag's gardens, the very crops of the green fields, the forests beyond, the singing river, *the children!* How could all that be weighed in the balance against him—one man—and come out wanting? How in the world could it be so?

Nevertheless, as the carriage stopped moving she pushed the door open eagerly. As she had hoped, they had spied her coming—yes, there were the little ones running to meet her! She gathered them into her arms, amid flurries of kisses and caresses, breathless endearments, and tight, clinging hugs. She could not get enough of them; she refused to allow Izzy to herd them away but drew them into the front, sunny sitting room with her, and spread out the gifts, all the little treasures she had brought for them. And while they devoured the toys and tins filled with goodies, Flora was content to lean back and observe them. Rory, though only four, took care to share with his sister and protect her interests. In fact, opening a box of caramels he handed the first one to her, and she rewarded him with a sticky kiss on the top of his head.

"We missed you, Mother," he said, glancing toward Flora. "You were gone away a long time." Remembering something unhappy, his face clouded over and he dropped the toy he had been playing with to come over beside her and place his hand in her lap.

"Uncle Gavin came and said that you had been naughty, and we should not call you mother, and if you didn't behave—" Tears choked his voice and dimmed his blue eyes.

Flora drew him to her breast with a cry. "Shame on Uncle Gavin. He had no right to frighten you." She lifted his face and looked into his eyes, willing him to feel and understand her meaning. "Uncle

Gavin is not a happy man, and sometimes he says things that are not true. Do you understand?"

The small face nodded solemnly.

"I am your mother, and I will always love you. You need not be afraid of anything anyone tells you."

The child placed his small, slender hands on her cheeks and kissed her. Flora felt tears of misery and foreboding fill her own eyes. Summoning all her energies of self-control, she sat on the floor and played with the children until their fears were all laughed away and they were drowsy and content enough to be carried off for their naps. Only then did she turn her attentions to the weighty problems Gavin's pride and greed were creating.

She sent for her mother to come to her. When Rowena bustled into the room she began defending herself like a nervous child who has not yet been accused. Flora waved her tumble of words aside.

"Gavin came here, obviously," Flora began, "and frightened the children. I want to know what he told you."

"Things that were hard to believe, daughter, things that made my heart sick, that—"

"Mother—what things?"

Rowena blinked a moment, struggling to order her thinking and draw forth something specific. Flora, watching the struggle, sighed.

"Let me tell you, briefly and plainly, Mother, what happened in Paisley. Anything beyond that is Gavin's anger and imaginings. Are you listening, Mother?"

Rowena nodded sullenly.

"I went to Paisley. I stayed in the home of Colin's brother and sister-in-law. I enjoyed their company, as well as his, enjoyed seeing the town, going to dinner, doing things young people do. One particular afternoon I attended a Mormon meeting, a large Mormon meeting with hundreds of people—a nice, quiet meeting."

Rowena could not contain herself. "You at such a place, my own daughter! Seen before hundreds, duped by these people who lie to the workers and urge them to revolt. They will turn business topsy-turvy, and what will men like your brother do then?"

Flora clenched her hands at her sides. "Mother, how blind you are! Men like Gavin oppress their workers and squeeze every bit of profit they can out of the blood and sweat of the working people. Mormons are peaceable; they encourage obedience and modesty and temperance."

Rowena shook her head, a slight, helpless gesture that maddened Flora.

"Did you know that your son went about threatening and bullying people—that he threatened me, marching into the house of one of the wealthiest and most respected of his competitors and making childish and wicked demands?"

"Flora, he was frightened, he was overcome with shame! Why are you doing this thing? You risk our happiness and security by associating with such people."

"Mother, haven't you heard a word I've been saying?"

Rowena blinked up at her through tear-dimmed eyes. "You were ever a strange one, Flora," she sighed. "This proves it. We are only protecting you from your own self. Gavin knows best. You must come to your senses and forsake this madness—"

Flora heard no more; she stormed from the room, knowing she must leave before she began to scream at the top of her lungs or shake that shocked, silly look from her mother's face. She fled to the gardens, trying to walk off her anger. "What am I to do? What am I to do?" she moaned. Injustice stung her like nothing else did, especially when turned against *her! Nevertheless,* she argued, *I am a grown woman. And Ravenwood belongs solely to me—bless Grandmother for that! Gavin will cool off, things will settle down, be forgotten. And I can still go my way. I have a right to, as much right as any other.*

But when she reentered the house she was still in a dark, thoughtful mood. She noticed that Nathan Forbes was in the sitting room soothing her mother; she did not envy him the task. *Thank heaven I had Great Grandmother to pattern after,* she thought. *What sort of self-respect would I have if there had been none but my mother to gauge my own life by?*

With an inescapable sense of sadness she climbed the stairs to her room, mourning, without realizing it, the loss of the old, idle peace she had once enjoyed.

Colin's note arrived ten days after her dismal homecoming; to Flora it seemed ten weeks, ten years. There was to be a baptism in the River Cart, between Paisley and Dumbarton, she read. It would please him immensely if she could contrive a way to attend. He would not guarantee, nor state it absolutely, but there was a great possibility that Kenneth would be one of the candidates baptized that day. Friday next, seven o'clock in the evening. Dared he entertain the sweet hope of seeing her there?

Flora smiled at his rhetoric. A Mormon baptism. She probably would have declined, but Kenneth, perhaps Janet—she *wanted* to be there in that case.

For the first few days after making her decision she deferred telling her mother. But, in thinking it over, she concluded that such behavior was stupid and cowardly. She would have to give some explanation for her journey. Did she wish to begin lying now? For, in these matters, one lie would lead to another, and soon there would be no end to it. Best to face it straight on and dismiss it for what it was: a simple, innocent activity. So she announced her intentions at dinner one night. The serving girl, ladling the soup, paused in midair and glanced up at Rowena. Flora felt her stomach muscles tighten, and nervously she picked at the nail on her thumb.

"That would be a most unwise thing to do, Flora." Her mother's stern voice had no power to it, and she resorted to her usual whine. "Don't start this again, Flora. How could you, just when I had begun to relax and thought perhaps we could all be at peace."

"We *can* be at peace. What in the world is preventing us?"

"You and your vain, foolish ways! Your stubborn refusal to—"

"Refusal to what, Mother? Let Gavin, from his ivory tower, dictate my life?" She was shouting, and she didn't want to. She struggled to control the pitch and tone of her voice. "I do not believe this—your willful blindness, your support of Gavin. Mother, what have I done?"

The pathetic appeal in her voice rendered her mother's arguments useless. Rowena put her hand to her head. "I've a raging headache now, Flora. Be a good girl and ask Izzy to make up her special chamomile brew. You ought to take some yourself, dear, and settle down a little."

So the encounter fizzled out, with no ending, no resolution, only a fresh set of wounds, a wider gap between her spirit and her mother's spirit, a deeper and drearier emptiness for her to walk in, alone.

When Flora went to her room to pack on the morning of her departure she stood dumbfounded before a bare, empty closet. She had not a large and sumptuous wardrobe, it was true. But she did have sufficient, and she liked fine clothing, especially gowns she could ride in, and light lawn or linen morning dresses. It made no difference now. Not one was left her: not a frock, not a shawl, not a petticoat—nor was there one pair of shoes. Nothing save what she wore on her body. She laughed outright at the apparent ridiculousness of it, then went in search of an explanation, for she could think of none whatsoever.

She found her mother alone in the front sunny parlor where she often sat with her sewing of a morning. When Rowena did not raise her eyes nor smile a greeting as her daughter entered, Flora merely said gently, "Mother, this is a ridiculous thing. Whose idea was it to pilfer my clothing?"

"We are saving you from yourself, Flora. One day you will thank us."

"And who are *we*, Mother?"

No reply whatsoever; just the click of her knitting needles, moving in, moving out.

"I am going to the baptism, and I want my clothes returned immediately. This is infantile, Mother."

"I can do nothing about it, Flora. Your things are not here, I can do nothing." Her hands trembled and she dropped a stitch. Flora turned and walked silently from the room. She knew her mother had spoken the truth. There was no help for her here. Of course, somehow, Gavin was behind this. Which meant he had a spy in her house. The idea made her want to laugh, but she knew it was not a laughing matter. Nor did she wish to suspect every face she met in the corridors of Ravenwood. It wasn't like the old days, when a large staff of people served in and were supported by this one house. But she still had a gardener, a housekeeper, a cook, two maids of all work, farm workers, and the factor, of course. Nathan Forbes. She had always liked Nathan, and she believed he liked her. Cook was too simple—old Arthur?—it could be *anyone!* What a terrible feeling to live with! Perhaps sometime when her mother was relaxed, unsuspecting, Flora could get her to slip and reveal some clue, some hint.

Meanwhile—meanwhile, she would attend the baptism just as she was! These Mormons were an unpretentious lot, that much she knew. No one would judge her, and all would understand if she explained; in fact, they would probably fancy her noble—that made her smile, too. What would Colin think? Oh, it would be worth it—anything would be worth it—just to see him, just to look into his eyes and feel the warmth of his voice, like a caress, speaking her name. She would go. She would show all of them, Gavin especially. In time he would have to tire of such petty manipulations, find better things to do with his time. Without saying a word to anyone, she went back upstairs to prepare for her journey as best she could.

So Kenneth had meant it; he was truly doing this, and Janet as well. Quiet Janet, was she doing this to please him? Flora wished she could ask. But Janet and Kenneth stood aside with the others who were to be baptized, each one dressed in white, each looking delicate somehow, ethereal, as if for the moment the spirit was a shining, more corporeal thing than the flesh. Flora kept glancing at those who were standing apart—those, the sanctified. She tried to laugh at herself. "Commitment on any level is frightening," Colin had once said to her, "and commitment to anything this demanding . . ." Yet the faces of the people standing before her seemed peaceful and sure.

A Mormon baptism. Not by sprinkling over an infant's head, but as they claimed the Savior had been baptized—and the scriptures bore their claims out—by immersion. Here, where low branches trailed in the swift, living water, their thick green leaves edged with autumn's first faint yellow. Elder Ramsey and Elder Burgess were here to perform the baptisms. First there was a hymn sung and a prayer offered. In the soft silence that followed, Flora noticed several heads turning with quick, anxious glances behind them.

"What is it, Colin?"

"I hope nothing at all. Several of those to be baptized work in your brother's factory, and we have heard rumors that he and others will not allow the ordinance to take place."

Flora felt herself shiver as the river breeze lifted the wet leaves. The first person stepped out from among the others and took Elder Ramsey's hand. *Elder. Brother and Sister.* It was strange, the manner in which they addressed one another. *Priesthood. Ordained power to baptize*—so many thoughts ran round her head.

"How do your parents feel about what Kenneth is doing?" She watched, interested to see Colin's response.

He took a moment to answer her. "They respect his right to make his own choices. I believe they may be concerned—but not disapproving."

"But they wouldn't say so, if they were."

"That's true, they would not. But I think I would feel it. Kenneth's become quite a changed man, you know."

"No, I don't know. In what ways?" They were whispering now, and Flora leaned closer, wanting to hear his answer. But they waited and bowed their heads while Brother Ramsey raised his arm and spoke the brief words, ending with: "In the name of the Father, and of the Son, and of the Holy Ghost. Amen." The woman slipped under the water, as smooth and still as the wet leaves that trailed there, and came up with a smile on her face, a glowing expression.

"It is not easy to explain, Flora," Colin continued. "He is more serious, more patient. He seems happier. And he thinks things through, judging them against different standards than he had before."

"Couldn't that just be part of growing up? Look at your father. He's both wise and kind. He didn't need Mormonism to make him that way."

"Flora, Flora." Colin looked truly concerned, but the next baptism was about to begin, and then the next, and then it was Janet's and Kenneth's turn, and they did not resume talking again.

Twenty people; an impressive number of converts. They were nearly half through when the gentle peace of the scene was disturbed by a sudden crashing in the undergrowth, the sound of men's voices, the stamp and whinny of horses. Flora could feel the blood drain from her face. She felt more fear than she would like to admit.

"Not real trouble, Colin!" she whispered. "Not here, at such a time."

But the noises, loud and purposeful, grew closer. Elder Ramsey held up his hand, and the silence which had already existed grew absolute. Flora could hear herself breathe. Then a sudden thought struck her with terror. *Gavin knows I was planning to come here. He orchestrated what happened back at Ravenwood. What might he do now?*

Those who had already been baptized stood with blankets wrapped round them, close together, like wet, dripping lambs. Elder Ramsey came up with long strides from the riverbank and planted himself at the head of the group, legs spread, arms folded across his broad chest. The intruders entered the quiet grove with a burst of sound that was grating, almost obscene to Flora's ears. The waves in the river seemed to rock from the shock of the noise; the low-hanging leaves rustled in protest. The men, heavy booted, some carrying riding whips, some stout sticks, seemed to level everything that stood in their way. But, when they came to Elder Ramsey, they stopped. He spoke not a word, asked not a question; they would be forced to make the first move. Several of the men shouted terrible things out, so that for a moment Colin covered Flora's ears with his hands. Then their ranks parted slightly to admit one tall, jaunty fellow with a red beard and red hair, and a red glow of hate in his dark eyes.

Gavin Douglas assumed his own bold stance and took his time

looking around. Then, pointing with his stick from place to place, he barked, "You—Taggart, you—Williamson, MacKellar, and Hay— you're dismissed. Don't show up for work tomorrow, and there'll be no severance pay."

Not a word greeted his harsh pronouncement. The leaves stirred, the river waves lapped at the shore. Gavin's eyes said: *Well?* He became confused and disoriented for a moment, then he regained the cold sneer of command and swung half-round, threatening with his stick as he spoke.

"Lewis, Gilchrist, Kirkpatrick—I'll give you a minute by the clock to decide. You go through with this stupidity, this defiance, and you may join your friends in the poorhouse." He pulled his gold watch from his breast pocket and glared down at it. The seconds ticked by. In the terrible silence they could hear his clock marking time. "Well, what say you?" he growled.

No one moved; not a foot, not a hand, not a facial muscle stirred. "Don't be fools, men! Can't you see I'm giving you a chance here?"

From among the white-clad figures a man stepped forward and walked toward Flora's brother, his head hanging down, as a man would walk to his own execution.

"Huntly!" The word was a syllable of triumph in Gavin's hard mouth. "I didn't spy you there. Good man! This will not be forgotten." He spun round, grinning. "Come now, the rest of you. Come to your senses."

Deep, terrible silence again. With a decisive click he closed the case on the watch and slipped it back into his pocket. "So be it, then. Live with your folly. Eat and drink it, it's all you'll get for a while."

His words seemed a signal for the sneers and ugly oaths to begin again. Some of the men who had come with Gavin, tired of hanging back patiently, began to poke at those standing nearest them with their thick sticks. One slid his under Flora's curly brown locks and lifted them with a shout of derision. "Hey, Gavin, look what we got here!"

Gavin turned, and when he saw her he seemed to leap forth, with a vengeance in his eyes that struck her motionless. He put his hand to her throat and pressed cold, bruising fingers into her flesh. "You refuse to learn, Flora! What does it take to convince you?" He shoved her from him with a hard thrust that sent her sprawling, and turned to address the man who had grabbed his free arm and twisted it, and whose fist was within an inch of his jaw. But the arching stick struck first, caught Colin square in the face, and he staggered back with a groan.

Flora, dazed, felt strong arms close round her, tight as a vise, and half lift, half drag her through the woods to where horses stood in a circle. Her captor handed her up to a man who sat in a saddle, waiting. She heard Gavin's voice.

"Take her to Ravenwood. Deposit her there."

Flora's skin crawled as the man's arms closed round her. This was Fergus Davidson, one of her brother's foremen at the mill; she had met him before. His body smelled of tobacco and stale whiskey. She cringed from the press of his arm against her. It would be a long, dark ride home.

But she could not think of herself. She could think of nothing but that little knot of people, solemn and still, submitting themselves to the rage and injustice of petty men. Submission to hardship—the light from within—she had seen it in the eyes of the white clad figures. *Colin,* her heart cried, *please! Please take care of me, please help me know what it is I should do.*

19

Fergus Davidson pushed his mount and in just over four hours they topped the rise above Ravenwood. The moon was a great round orb spilling light, so that the graceful gray walls stood out in eerie relief against the darker stretch of black sky. Fergus did "deposit her" there, with no ceremony; merely a rough push to help her down to the ground. She steadied herself with a hand on the horse's lathered neck for a moment, then he spurred off. It was near midnight. She stood in the drive long after the scatter of his horse's hooves through the loose pebbles had died to an echo, and the only sound was the wind, welcoming her home, easing the strains of travel with its cool, kindly breath.

It was strange what Ravenwood meant to her. Strange that Anne, a poor country girl, an unlanded farmer's daughter, should have merged her spirit so closely with this place that it was her blood, the female line, who had ever since stood to inherit. Perhaps fate deemed it so. Were not women the hoarders, the ones who held on, who loved and remembered with fierce loyalty? Surely the woman's heart was the center of any home worth living in. At least with Macpherson and Douglas women it had always been so.

Flora was cold and hungry, but she did not feel tired; her spirit was too stirred up to rest. After washing herself and finding something to eat from Bess's ample larder, she sat in the long, shadowed library, smelling the polished wood and leather mingled with the musty pungency of old books. Even Morag's gardens did not hold the same peace this room held. She leaned back and closed her eyes, feeling strangely fulfilled, and somehow not all alone, as she ofttimes did in this place.

At first the light rapping at the door did not stir her; it sounded no louder than the wind with its usual disturbances. Then suddenly her eyes flew open and she knew someone was there. She lit a candle and walked out to the entranceway.

"Who is it?" she whispered through the lock. The hour was very late and everyone else in the household was long abed. She had too vivid an impression of the scene she had only hours ago passed through to not shudder a bit as she slid the bolt back and held the light high so that she might see who stood there.

The face before her was one she recognized instantly, though the wide forehead was smeared with blood and the eyes were wild. "Elder Ramsey!"

He held his finger up to his lips.

"No one is awake here," she assured him.

"I am not alone," he whispered. "There are four of us, Flora—four of us beaten, driven out, and pursued. I am afraid we need someplace to hide."

Her reply came without thinking, without effort or doubt "The heather cottage," she said. "Wait here a minute. I'll be right back."

She grabbed the ring of keys from their peg in the kitchen, as well as Morag's old cape. The wind had grown colder; it whined about the chimney stones. "Follow me, through the gardens," she told Elder Ramsey. "It isn't far."

As the key turned in the lock with a grating of protest she realized she had not been to the cottage since Emily died. She and Emily used to bring the two babies out here, and while they played on the floor the sisters, like older children, sang their favorite songs, giggling, sometimes acting silly, while Emily played the harpsichord. There was a new spinet in the formal sitting room of the great house, but this harpsichord had a sound like nothing else they had ever heard, and it drew them both.

"Do you think it wicked, perhaps sacrilegious, to play it?" Emily had asked the first time they dared.

Flora had shaken her head thoughtfully. "I don't believe so. Other women have played it, living women like us." And Emily had such a delicate touch with the keyboard, she could draw out the feeling that hovered beneath the notes by the pressure she applied and the length and stress of each sound she created.

But when death came and snatched Emily—so singing with life, so vital, so *needed*—then memories of the harpsichord haunted Flora's mind. *Perhaps there is a spell or curse on the old instrument, perhaps I set her death in motion by telling her: "Yes, it's all right, go ahead."*

Such thoughts had plagued her, stirred her raw emotions into eddies of guilt and pain. And she had wept when they buried Emily and the harpsichord did not speak. She knew it was accusing her with its silence. And then her father had died, taken in much the same, un-expected manner. Flora thought then: *This is my punishment, to have the two people I loved most taken, to have nothing but pain left.*

Of course, Rory and Lilias, lovely as little cherubs, had changed that. They were not only someone to love, they loved her in return.

With an effort she shuddered off all thought as she welcomed the weary, shivering men into the cottage. Draped over chairs were a few rugs and old blankets, which she urged the men to wrap themselves in, but the interior of the cottage was amazingly warm, albeit musty from having been shut up for so long. In the shadows of the corner sat the old sofa—what stories she had heard as a child about all that had taken place in that corner! She looked up, and Elder Ramsey was watching her.

"I can find food for you," she offered, "and water to wash in. And perhaps even dry shirts."

He shook his head. "I do not wish to endanger you further."

"Nonsense." She threw her head back. "This is my home—literally. Will you come with me and help me carry things back?"

He complied, and Flora moved quickly and efficiently. Despite her bravado, she did feel afraid. And that very fear angered her, so that her whole being was awhirl with unwholesome emotions. As they neared the edge of the gardens and approached the heather cottage, Elder Ramsey put his hand on her arm.

"Flora, you are an angel of mercy, and your Heavenly Father is mindful of you."

His words, with their different, unaccustomed accent, sent a most uncommon thrill through her, a feeling of warmth and light. She paused and smiled up into his solemn brown eyes. *Do you truly think so?* she wanted to ask. *How can you say such things with that air of ab-solute assurance you have?*

"He'll grant your righteous desires, Flora. Be still. Trust in him and feel the joy he desires for you."

"I will try," she breathed, feeling already a lightness of spirit, a loosening of the binding emotions she had been struggling against. She put her hand over his. "Did my brother hurt Colin after they dragged me away?" She thought she saw his expression alter; she could feel him hesitate. "Is Colin all right?"

"Your brother caught him full in the face with a blow of his stick. He has a long, nasty cut along his forehead, but I don't believe his nose is broken. He'll be all right." He heard her sigh, felt her go tense, and shook the arm he held. "Colin's a strong, plucky lad, girl. I tell you, he's fine."

"Did he try to fight back? I can't bear to think of him hurt!"

"Don't fret yourself about Colin. If Gavin had struck you, he'd have gone into the fray with no thought whatsoever. But he is not generally unwise or hasty."

"Why?" Flora cried. "Why do men like my brother enjoy hurting people? Gavin was never like that before. A bit mean, centered on his own desires, but not this, not cruel. It frightens me."

"Well it might," he replied softly. "Evil will take all the help it can get, lass, and men like your brother play right into Satan's hands."

"How do you mean?"

"I mean Satan desires to thwart the work, to see mankind in misery and bondage, so he uses men's own fears and weaknesses against them."

Flora thought she understood that. "And the social conditions in our overcrowded cities are threat enough to men like Gavin, without Mormonism coming along to worsen things."

"Yes. Enlightenment is always threatening, overwhelming in its insecurities and demands. Truth has always had the narrow path to walk, now, hasn't it, lass? The narrow, exacting way."

They went back into the cottage and dispersed the food and clothing. Flora wished she might linger and talk, but she asked only, "How long will you be wanting to stay?"

"Just until morning. We can catch a train then."

"And leave?" she cried.

"We'll go to Edinburgh for a few weeks. We'll not only protect ourselves that way, but keep others from suffering on our account." His voice was low and sympathetic. "Things will die down, lass. We are not abandoning anything; the work will go on."

"Sister Douglas, did you know this cottage was being used as a clothes dump?" one of the men said, laughter in his voice. He held up a fine, flounced petticoat. "Looks like this might fit you."

"My clothes!" Flora cried with sudden comprehension.

"Back here, behind the couch in the corner."

Sure enough, all her things were there, dumped unceremoniously, and probably hastily. *Who possesses a key to this cottage?* she thought. *Who is in league with my brother?*

She explained the situation. It was something they could all laugh over, after the far worse scenes they'd been through.

"I'll come for them in the morning," Flora said, feeling suddenly sleepy. "You men need some rest. Haste ye back, now." She smiled gently at the kind, tired faces. "And God go with you and protect you," she breathed as she slipped out into the cool, restless night air. But the restlessness in her own spirit had waned. Peace enfolded her as she walked through the dark fragrance toward the bulk of Ravenwood House. Peace and a subtle sense of well-being which helped her sleep well that night.

Next morning when she went to the cottage to collect her clothes and lock the door, the men had already gone. She tidied up a bit and loaded her belongings into a wheelbarrow lined with a clean blanket. She wondered what anyone seeing her would think; she wondered whose spying eyes would curse her discovery. Should she distrust the whole lot of them, and be safe that way? One of the girls, hanging clothes on the line, was singing. And so were the late summer birds. The cool touch of the September air was invigorating; it seemed too lovely a day to admit anger or cruelty, lies or deceptions.

Nevertheless, once she had her clothes brushed out, hung, and folded carefully, with everything in its place, she went in search of Nathan and demanded his cottage key from him. He removed it from his ring and gave it to her with a long quiet look, but no questions. The ring which had hung trustingly on the kitchen hook for as long as she could remember she now kept on a belt round her waist. Other than that, she made no fuss at all. No one would know what she was about, and certainly not what she was thinking.

Right now all her thoughts were for Colin. She wrote a long note to him and rode into the village to post it herself. While there she noticed Nathan Forbes coming out of the constable's office. He carried something, a packet or a book, in his hands. When he looked up and spied her, he slipped the bundle inside his coat, lowered his eyes, and hurried off in the other direction. The tight feeling returned, and her heart began to beat faster. Instinctively she glanced all around. Had her guests of last night been apprehended? Had they been spied on— was Nathan reporting their whereabouts to an interested constable? *No!* she stopped herself. *Don't let your imagination create trouble where none may exist!* There could be half a dozen sane, normal explanations for what she had just seen.

She rode home and spent the remainder of the day with the children. In the evening, after reading bedtime stories and tucking them in for the night, she went down to the library and drew Colin's copy of the Book of Mormon from the back of the low drawer where she had secreted it. She had not opened its cover for weeks. She read it now with a hunger she had never felt before, and every word that she read sunk into her mind and spirit with more meaning, more purpose than it had the first time. She felt like a dry sponge receiving a cool, sweet rain of water. She drank the pages hungrily. But the satisfaction she experienced did not alleviate the feeling of need: the more she drew in, the more she desired.

She read far into the night, until the big house had gone still around her, and nothing spoke but the clock, keeping a steady, unquestioning rhythm, as if it were the heartbeat of the dark, ancient house. And the rhythm was hers. The house seemed to breathe with her, sigh with her, hold its breath as she dropped to her knees, bent her head on her arms, and prayed.

20

_____

The following Sunday Flora attended the scheduled Presbyterian services at the old kirk with her mother and the children. She considered herself a regular churchgoer, missing only in times of illness or bad weather. She had wanted Emily's bairns raised with religion, raised to know the hymns and the psalms and the *feel* of spiritual things—things which she had known as a child. This was one of her great-grandmother's legacies Flora would not forsake. But this particular morning the sermon seemed unaccustomedly dull and narrow. She fidgeted in her seat. She found her mind coming up with questions, differing interpretations, deeper meanings than the staid, grayhaired minister intoned. She sat back against the hard seat with a sigh. For generations Macphersons and then Douglases had worshipped here. The very wood of the place was imbued with their spirit, as the flesh of a man is imbued with his spirit. *Will all that come to an end with me?* The question startled her, frightened her.

As if in answer, early in the afternoon a carriage pulled up to the door. Peering out of the window, she recognized it at once, and her heart gave a leap. Not concerning herself with propriety, she ran out to greet Colin. He gathered her into his arms. Oh, the fresh, clean scent of him! The feel of his hands on her face and his lips touching hers! She stood back to survey him; the scar on his forehead, though partially covered by his thatch of black hair combed across it, still looked red and unhealed. She touched it gingerly. "Colin—" Then she buried her face against his shoulder, ashamed for what her brother had done.

"Don't concern yourself with trivialities, Flora," he murmured, his voice low and tender. "He has caused no permanent damage, and you and I have so much for which to be happy."

She smiled through blurred eyes and let him lead her away from her gloomy thoughts. In fact, he led her into the garden, sat her on a bench over which the sun scattered yellow ducats through the low-trailing branches of a hawthorn. There, where the pungent fragrance of lavender hung like a benediction, he spoke words Flora had never believed would be spoken to her.

"I love you, Flora," he said. "With my whole being I love you, and wish to spend my life with you, my eternities with you."

Joy leaped up in her, like a melody of gladness. She wanted to laugh, but she could feel tears in her eyes.

"Will you marry me, Flora? Will you be my wife, and allow me the privilege of caring for you, loving you, serving you—"

She placed her finger on his lips. "Yes, my darling," she whispered. And if he had not leaned over to kiss her, she would have burst into tears. She had known the love of a father, the devotion of a sister, but she had never imagined the happiness, cleansing and sweeping, and all-encompassing, that surged through her now. She trembled in her amazement, not wanting to lose one breath, one heartbeat, one sigh. Could such happiness be real? Could it endure? Could it become a day-to-day thing, so that one basked in it always, even took it for granted? "Colin," she whispered, "you will not change your mind?"

He might have laughed at her, but he heard the fears she would have kept hidden, and so he drew her close to him, his arm gently encircling her. "You will lose breath before I stop loving you." He spoke the words slowly, so that she felt the caress of them settle into her heart. "Was I not led to you? Did my spirit not recognize yours, cry out to you—call your name without knowledge of it? What greater assurance do you need? The world will stop turning, cease to exist, before I cease to love you."

Her heart believed him. She could not do otherwise. There, with only peace and beauty as companions, they planned their dreams, drawing out those secret longings which love alone has the power to unlock and reveal.

Perfection cannot hold court for long, not in mortal affairs. The first ripple, the first mar upon the pure surface came later that night when they walked hand in hand along the river and Colin said simply, "I wish to be baptized, Flora. I truly do."

"Baptized—you mean you wish to become a Mormon, live the way Mormons live?"

"Yes, I do."

Fear gripped her insides, but she drew a deep breath and said nothing.

"I've watched what it's done for Kenneth and Janet. And others. I want the same happiness and purpose in my life"—he paused ever so briefly—"in ours."

She hedged. "How has it been of late? Are my brother and his like still stirring up trouble?"

"We took the wind out of their sails some by finding places in our mills for the men they dismissed. And we've avoided proselyting among their workers, at least given it a breathing spell. Why, the elders have gone off to Edinburgh. Brother Grant's been in charge of the meetings since they left. Did you know that?"

"I did." She explained to him how she knew, told of her adventure the night of their rude parting, and he listened with interest, his eyes twinkling. "You've got more spirit, lass, than you know. And to think that, for your pains, you discovered your stolen clothing! Serves Gavin right, doesn't it?" He looked off toward the cottage with a thoughtful expression. "I'm sure Elder Ramsey blesses your name."

"He does—he did. He's a wonderful man, Colin. I think highly of him."

Colin nodded agreement. He had a way of drawing her out. Before she knew it she was telling him of the things she'd been reading, how different her responses were this time.

"Have you been praying about the things you've been reading?" he asked outright.

She winced a little, but nodded.

"I do not wish to push you or hurry you," he responded, watching her eyes. "But this is surely one thing we must come to grips with, come to some sort of agreement upon, you and I."

If we are to be married—if a marriage between us is to prosper. He did not say the words, but they sat there, hung in the air like a little dark cloud that sent cold chills up her spine. "I'm not sure I know—have a testimony, or whatever they call it." She realized how weak her words sounded, and she wished she could recall them.

"Keep praying," Colin urged, his voice kind, nonjudgmental. "Let love show you the way."

It was a strange thing to say, and she remembered it after he left her. She had been taught: God is love. As though love were a source, God a source, something unseen, all-powerful. But the Mormons taught that God was also a Heavenly Father to man, that the priesthood power restored to the young prophet was *His* power, and that man and woman together could grow to become like this Heavenly Father.

It seemed too big to her, too overwhelming. She knew she was running away. But now Colin had made that impossible for her. He was anxious to be baptized, holding back only for her. How long would he wait? How long would he be patient? Should she do this thing for his sake, and gain her own conviction later? Surely Colin, with his strength and vivacity, could help that to happen. But would he notice what was lacking and be disappointed, having anticipated from her so much more?

So she reasoned through the quiet autumn days while she put the garden to rest, and the men brought in the last of the harvest, and she and her mother dried fruit and baked apple tarts for the children, and the days tasted crisp and delicious, and each one seemed a new gift.

So she reasoned and read, and prayed and pondered, until the smallpox struck, and her world turned into a bleak wasteland overnight.

It really happened that quickly. She had no time to prepare for it. One day Rory and Lilias were playing happily, chasing their pet rabbit round the garden, bare now in so many spots that he was easy to spy. That night Lilias woke from her sleep complaining that her head hurt. She was burning with fever. She was not to sleep the child's peaceful sleep again. When Rory awoke in the morning he, too, complained that his head ached and, though Izzy fed him a light breakfast, he could not keep it down.

Flora sent for Dr. Fletcher, who came in looking worn and rumpled as though he, too, had not slept. He shook his head solemnly before even examining the children, only pushing Lilias's golden curls back to reveal two small red spots on the side of her neck. "Smallpox," he pronounced, his face muscles twitching when he said it. "You must keep them apart from all other members of the household, and boil the utensils and dishes they eat with."

"And?" Flora looked down at the white, pinched little faces. Dr. Fletcher placed his large callused hand on the golden head.

"There is not much you can do for the bairns but try to keep them cool and as comfortable as possible. Bathe their bodies with cool cloths, see if you can get them to keep liquids down." He sighed, and lifted his hand as though the effort wearied him. "'Tis everywhere, lass. We've had several deaths in the village already, young tykes like these."

Death was commonplace to him, but to Flora a nightmare. She wanted to scream and gnash her teeth and frighten the spectre away.

Flora organized the household, assigning emergency duties to everyone, and posted a letter to Colin telling him what had happened. Then she forgot about everything and took over the care of the children herself, resting when she must in a low bed beside theirs in the nursery, serving their needs day and night, whenever their small voices called for her. At first it seemed Rory would suffer only a light case; he appeared always lucid and sometimes held down food and seemed to build a little strength after his attacks of chills and vomiting. But from the start Lilias was too frail to fight off the disease. She lay under her mother's old wool comforter, woven in soft shades of rose, and looked like a faded and wilting blossom herself. She seldom cried out or demanded attention, but lay curled in a small ball, whimpering like a new kitten, her gold hair dull and dampened with perspiration.

Flora could not bear to sit by and watch their sufferings. At times, when her mind teetered between rage and anguish, she would run away to the gardens and stumble along the dark paths, her way lit by the high, fitful moon. Only the night wind could wipe the suffering out of her and cleanse her enough to go on.

And she prayed. There was no one but God she could talk to, and she found herself addressing him as *Heavenly Father* the way the Mormons did, speaking as though he were someone familiar, to whom she could pour out her heart.

On the fifth day after the disease first struck, Lilias lapsed into a deep sleep, and she never woke up. Lying so still and pale, golden lashes brushing her white cheeks, she looked like an angel already. After a few hours she stirred once, her small body shuddered, and the breath that had lifted her narrow chest as a breeze stirs through rose petals sighed out of her suffering body and left her at peace. Rory heard Flora weeping and lifted his head from his pillow.

"Is my Lilias dead?" he asked.

"Oh, Rory," she cried, not wanting to answer him.

"She is, or you would not grieve so. Then I shall die, too." And from that moment it seemed he gave up the struggle and let the sores and fever and chills have their way.

Flora washed Lilias's fair limbs, no more substantial than a rag doll's, washed her limp hair, brushing it out into spinning gold ringlets that shimmered like a fairy's jeweled crown. They must bury her quickly; word had been sent to Gavin. He arrived with his wife only hours before the funeral. He stepped out of the carriage looking pale and solemn, and his dark eyes were lusterless and sad. Flora remembered the hate, black and ugly, that had burned in them the last time she had looked upon him, and she shuddered.

Poor Agatha. What must it be like for her to live with the man? She was a sweet thing, really, not greedy and pushy like Gavin, but easy to lead. And it seemed to Flora that Gavin loved her; perhaps in his private hours he showed as much. Did Agatha wish for children of her own yet? Flora had never heard her talk on the subject.

She would not allow them to embrace her. "I've had the care of the children," she explained. "You must protect yourselves."

When Gavin gazed down upon the dead child a great shudder shook through him; he leaned back against a chair for support. "She looks just like Emily did when we were children. I cannot bear it!" he cried. Flora, watching him, thought suddenly, *He does still have a heart, something yet has power to touch him, even if it is his own suffering.* But she wanted desperately to cry out, to open her arms to him and comfort his bright head on her shoulder, the way she had so often when he was a boy.

As they stood by the open grave, a mere dark slash in the green sod, and the pipes wailed over the chill air, he turned to Flora with tears in his eyes. "'Tis a piteous thing, sister. I am sorry for your sake, Flora, sorry she's been taken from you." With her gloved hand she reached out for his and clung to it, lest the tears that ached in her throat betray her.

Gavin and Agatha drove back to Paisley that same day, and the other guests in turn mercifully faded into the dull gray expanse that the hours of this day had become. Dr. Fletcher gave Flora's mother a sedative to calm her. Bit by bit the tight winding of the demanding hours loosened and slowed.

At last Flora walked up the stairs wearily, leaning heavily on the banister for support, and softly entered the lonely nursery. A single light burned on a low table, illuminating the tear-stained face of the small boy she called her son. She dropped down onto her knees beside him.

"So you have taken Lilias home to you, Emily," she whispered. "I do not begrudge you that, though she was a light, a light in our lives, just as you were. But one is enough! Leave me something, for mercy's sake!"

She felt a hand on her shoulder and stumbled to her feet with a cry. Elder Ramsey was standing above her. "Colin told me," he whispered. "I came as fast as I could."

She felt no comprehension of what he was saying, why he had come to her.

"Would you like me to administer to the child, Flora, and petition Heavenly Father to spare his life?"

Of course! The elders of the Church had been given authority to lay their hands on the head of the sick, to pronounce a blessing of healing. She had heard people talk of such healings; she knew it had been done in these parts before.

"In the household of faith," Elder Ramsey said, drawing her hands up. "Have you faith, Sister Flora, that God, if he so desires, has the power to heal this lad?"

Into her mind came the words of the first Mormon preaching she'd heard—Elder Ramsey preaching, speaking the teachings of Joseph, the Prophet. *"By faith all things exist, by it they are upheld. Faith is the first great governing principle which has power, dominion, and authority over all things."*

"I understand," she answered. And she did. "I know this can be done." Her eyes said: *You have your faith and now I, too, have mine.*

Colin entered the room. She should have known he would come to her! When he bent to kiss her she motioned him away. "I do not wish to endanger you," she explained, but his eyes grew almost angry and he gathered her into his arms.

Then, with oil consecrated to the purpose, the Mormon elder anointed the small sleeping head and laid his hands protectingly, lovingly upon the child. Elder Ramsey spoke like an angel, and each word thrilling through her was like a pinprick of light. And Flora knew, she knew that God would honor this man's petition; she knew it was heaven's kind will that this one remaining child live.

As Elder Ramsey said amen and lifted his hands, the boy stirred. His thin eyelids fluttered, then opened. He looked at Flora. "Say good-bye to Lilias, Mother," he said, his voice weak and raspy. "She's waiting for you over there."

Slowly Flora turned and looked in the direction the child indicated. She saw nothing but the lace curtain moving gently, as a breath of air lifted it. "Is she standing by the window?"

"Yes. Kiss your hand to her and tell her you love her, Mother, so she may go."

Blinded by tears Flora walked to the window. "Lilias," she whispered. "My love! Kiss your mother for me, and don't forget us—don't forget us down here!"

The window was open barely a crack; she pushed it wider and leaned out into the cool evening. She was crying openly now. But the music came, reaching through the dusk to comfort her, soft as a kiss from the lips of the fair child who had left her, pure as an unspoken prayer. She closed her eyes and let the music pour over her, through her, melody sweet as an angel's voice, playing on and on, until Colin's hands drew her gently away, and for the first time in a week her head touched her own pillow, and she slept, dreaming no dreams, but waking up with the music still sounding inside her head.

21

I wish to be baptized here, where the river runs through the woods above Ravenwood," Flora told Colin. Colin was glad to agree. He loved Ravenwood and had talked of giving up the mill entirely to become a gentleman farmer, or at the least spending summers there, keeping the place working, assuring that it would always be a part of their lives.

Flora hoped the baptism could be accomplished with little fuss, and quickly. Each day now the fingers of the frost crept father across the fields, and the river ran cold and deep. Flora thought she could do this and tell no one, not even her mother. After she and Colin were married they could attend Mormon meetings openly.

"And until then you will keep attending the village kirk?" Colin asked.

She had not given that consideration. "In truth, your name should no longer be on their records as a member," Colin added. She put her hands over her eyes at the thought.

"Do not distress yourself," Elder Ramsey comforted gently. "Your name will be engraven in the Lamb's book of life."

"Kenneth and Janet should be here when we are baptized," Colin urged.

"No, they will understand," Flora argued. "I should like Rory to be there, too. But that would require too much time, waiting while he grows well and strong enough. And if we wait, if Gavin somehow gets word, if he is given the chance to spoil things . . ."

They thought through all the conditions carefully, and all three gathered in Morag's quiet library and knelt in prayer together. And on the following morning, when the sky was still rose stained and the sun's tentacles tangled like gold tendrils in the high tree branches, Colin and Flora dressed in white clothing and met Elder Ramsey, who was also attired in white.

The morning was pure. Flora felt pure as she walked, her hand warm within Colin's, all within her still and at peace. They walked far into the woods, where they could be free of the fear of detection. Here a sweet spirit prevailed. Here she could think of Emily and Lilias and believe what Elder Ramsey had assured her was reality, that she would see them again, be reunited with them as a family—all suffering over, all joy restored. And in the hush they knelt together and invoked heaven's blessings to linger with the spirit of the ancient woods and the innocent chatter of linnet, lark, and thrush.

Flora watched Elder Ramsey lead Colin down into the water. Their movements were deliberate, their expressions unhurried and peaceful, but Colin's eyes shone. Flora could feel his happiness extending out from him, much as the ripples of water circled outward, gently dampening the thin, thirsty soil of the shore. Her heart was still as she watched, and she felt her own spirit one with them.

When it came her turn she stepped down into the river with no hesitation, though the sharp chill took her breath away. As she shut her eyes and felt the water close round her she saw her great-grandmother's face, not Lilias or Emily as she had anticipated. And the strange thing was that Morag appeared young. Her hair was thicker and darker than Flora's, her brown eyes filled with light, tender and laughing.

She came up spitting water, her teeth chattering despite her determination to ignore the wet and the cold. Colin draped a warm blanket around her and kissed the top of her head. They walked back with more speed and less conversation than they had come out with. When they arrived at the house the chimneys were smoking, the maids would be at their work by now. But perhaps her mother still lay safely abed.

Flora went into her room and changed her wet clothing, then peeked in on Rory, who was sleeping soundly and appeared to be breathing evenly. Anxious, she hastened down to the library where she had told the two men to meet her. No one was yet in the room when she walked inside. But she felt something, almost a presence, something quiet and tender. *I can be patient,* she thought. *The time for waiting will be short now. Colin and I have done the right thing, and we love one another.*

The words came into her mind as though someone had spoken them, with absolute clarity: *"Perfect love casteth out fear."* She smiled to herself and repeated them. *One can hear something one's whole life,* she thought, *believe it, understand it, but experience alone makes it real.*

This was the last benediction, this lightening of fear from her spirit, this calm joy inside.

She was able to kiss Colin and let him go, though the parting wrenched her. She was able to greet her mother, listen to her peevish complainings, and feel nothing but a gentle pity. And when she lifted Rory in her arms and carried him out for a walk round the cold gardens, she thought: *Joy feels too much like pain. All-tender, all-consuming, too much for the frail mortal soul to contain.*

The eyes that watched her marked her every movement, her every mood. But Flora was blissfully unaware of them. She went her way in a protective shell of love, which kept all that was ugly, all that was petty or evil, away.

A week passed. She was to go to be with Colin at the week's end. Rory would be strong enough to leave behind, in her mother's and Izzy's care, for a day or two. She would stay with Kenneth and Janet; they planned to all celebrate together. She had only two days left to wait.

Early Thursday afternoon a rider came down the path to the great house; Flora heard the loose stones strike and scatter at his passing. He was coming uncommonly fast. She opened the door and stood watching him, and recognized his face before he reached her.

"Kenneth!"

"Yes, it's Colin," he said with merciful speed, answering the question that choked in her throat. "An accident at the mill, and he was hurt." He groped for her cold fingers. "The doctors say he'll be all right, Flora, but he's asking for you."

She was calm. Like a person in a dream, she moved with deliberation, detachment. "Come rest yourself," she told Kenneth. "I'll order my father's gray gelding to be saddled; he's the fastest we have."

Where is Nathan? she thought, and turned to see him right at her elbow.

"I'll take care of everything, Miss Flora. We should saddle a fresh horse for Mr. Fraser." She nodded; she had not thought of that. "Put on something warm for the journey," he cautioned her. His voice sounded concerned, like a father's. But his bright eyes had narrowed, and he was watching her carefully. She turned and walked the stairs to her room, organizing in her mind the things she must do, the instructions she must leave, feeling nothing at all.

She still felt nothing when she slid, stiff and sore, from the saddle, and ran up the stairs leading to Ewen Fraser's big house. The old man himself greeted her, held out his arms to her. He smelled not unpleasantly of fragrant tobacco mixed with a gentleman's fine cologne. And his body, though thin and sparse of flesh, felt amazingly supple and strong. "Bless your heart, my dear. The lad'll be better now you're here."

She hurried up the steep stairs, tucking a stray curl behind her ear, not caring one bit how she looked, just needing to be with him, touch him, convince herself that he was alive and all right.

She entered the darkened room. Colin was half lying, half reclining, propped by pillows, but his eyes were closed. His skin was pasty and pale, and a fat bandage was wrapped round his head, looking stark against the tousled black locks of his hair.

"I hear you! I recognize that light footfall—and I can smell your perfume!" He opened his eyes and tried to smile at her, but their blue was dull and clouded, and she noticed that his lip looked swollen.

The accident, Kenneth had earlier explained, was an explosion which had gone off in one of the biggest spinning rooms in the early hours after opening, when all the looms were manned and busy. An explosion *set off*, Kenneth believed, because what other explanation was there? The room had been crammed full of people, and twelve workers had been injured, some seriously. Three of their new, very costly power looms were put out of commission entirely. Colin had just entered the room to examine a bolt of marred material one of the workers had reported.

There had been no time for questions, but the ride to Paisley gave Flora a long time in which to think. It seemed clear to her that it was a case of sabotage, and if sabotage, who else could it be but Gavin? So, with a sickness inside her, she went up to comfort the man she loved, who had nearly met his death at the hands of her only brother. And she trembled at the cruel ironies life held in store.

"I *am* all right, Flora!" Colin was saying. "Sit here beside me and tell me how your days have passed since I left you."

She noticed as she sank into a chair and pulled it close against the bedside that one of his arms was bandaged as well, the one he had held up to protect his face from the explosion. She tried to speak of light things: Rory's improvement, the new kitten Izzy's niece had brought for him, the storm which had split a huge limb off her favorite oak tree. But the common words mulled in her throat.

"I can't do this," she protested weakly, after a few moments. "I can't make the words come out."

"If you knew what your voice, just the sound of your voice, does for me, Flora!" he pleaded. "Say anything at all, speak nonsense, recite nursery rhymes—"

Just don't ask me about what happened! she thought, with a slow, weary anger. She leaned over and kissed his forehead. "All right, my poor darling," she whispered against his dark curls. And somehow she began speaking again. Not until the doctor came in nearly an hour later and convinced Colin to swallow some medication to help the pain and the swelling did she stop, even for a moment. Then he fell asleep holding her hand. And she sat there, reluctant to pry his fingers away from hers, until his mother entered the room and insisted that she get up and let Millie fix her something to eat, for she looked as if she might keel over and faint right there.

She ate and rested. When she awoke it was late in the evening; Colin was still asleep. Kenneth had gone home to his own house. Flora needed someone to talk to, she needed some of her questions answered, so she braved a request of Colin's mother. Did she happen to know where the Mormon missionaries lived? She did. She would even have the carriage brought round to take her, if Flora promised not to stay long. It was growing too late for a person to go visiting, much less a young lady alone. How motherly Jean appeared with her concerned, bustling ways! Just being near her made Flora realize how much she missed her great-grandmother's interest and care in her life.

Mr. Fraser's driver took her from Ferguslie, where the family lived, through Williamsburgh and Townshead, all "nice" areas where mill owners had homes and kept their mills, and was drawing dangerously close to Sneddon, one of the poor sections where many of the Irish immigrant workers lived, before he slowed the carriage to a stop and came round to open the door for her.

"This be it, lass," he said. "Second door on your left. I'll wait here for ye, but the missus says, don't be long."

She smiled and left him standing there, feeling suddenly reluctant. Elder Burgess answered her ring. "Come in, Sister Douglas," he smiled, but his voice was low, and he kept glancing behind him. As she seated herself he called into the back room, "We have a visitor, Brother."

Elder Ramsey came out slowly. His eyes looked dull, his face slightly puffed. She began to ask, "Are you ill?" but he jumped ahead of her. "You're here to inquire about the accident, Flora, I can see it in your eyes. Why do you assume *I* know everything, *I* have all the answers?"

She felt as though he had struck her; his voice was so harsh, so bereft of sympathy.

He continued: "Yes, it looks suspicious to me. And yes, I believe your brother had motives, more than one. First of all, one of his foremen, an Irishman, came to us and asked to be baptized, and who were we to deny him? Then, bold as the Irish be, he stood up and told Gavin Douglas what he had done. Your brother hit the ceiling and, of course, had to dismiss him to save his own face. Then the lad asked Colin for a position, and I advised Colin not to take him on, but of course he did. A hundred or more weaving firms in Paisley, and the Irishman would have to work for your brother!" He ran his fingers through his thick hair distractedly. "'Tis in part a simple matter of ill timing. All this took place the same week some of the mill owners held a big reform meeting—headed by Mr. Orr and Colin's father, of course. Then, heaven knows how, probably from the Irishman, your brother found out that both you and Colin had been baptized—"

Flora clapped her hand to her mouth. "And the place?"

"Ravenwood? Yes. I think he learned that, too."

Flora was now thoroughly consumed with her thoughts; she did not notice her friend's growing distraction and distress. He paced the room end to end, then planted himself squarely in front of her. "I've given you what you came for, Flora. I have matters of my own to see to. Now, please leave me. Go."

"I came for your advice, for your help," she protested.

"I have no help for you!" The words were a rude cry. Flora felt anger building in her and was forming a retort in her mind when she looked up and her glance caught his gaze—one brief heartbeat of raw, trembling anguish before he turned away.

"What is it?" she cried, rising and drawing close to him. "You have suffered something terrible. What is it?"

The silence trembled with his pain. She reached out her hand and touched him. "Please trust me," she said.

Still he fought the silence that encased his suffering. When he spoke, his voice was colorless, with no timbre in it. "I received word today that my wife died last month, died of the cholera. She has been buried these two weeks and more." He ran trembling fingers through his hair again. "She died calling for me." The words ended in a sob, which he choked back.

"No," Flora murmured, "no. Anything, dear God, but this!"

She turned him gently to face her, and put her arms around him. *It is not fair,* her heart cried. *He, who has blessed and succored so many, who has suffered so nobly and sweetly, who thinks of everyone save himself!*

He felt her sympathy and lowered his heavy head onto her shoulder. "She called for me, 'Malcolm! Malcolm!' Suffering, needing me! And I was not there! She died without me—and now He expects me to live without her."

She stood holding him, tears streaming down her cheeks. She was murmuring to him, without knowing she did so, and she called him by name. "Malcolm, Malcolm, my poor, dear, marvelous friend." She stroked his head soothingly, as she would have stroked Rory's. "My great-grandfather's name was Malcolm," she said, for some reason. "He knew what it meant to suffer. He fought in the rebellion of '45 and was wounded, but that was only the beginning. He saw his home burnt to the ground, his sister ravished by the soldiers, his father hung from the beam of his own house"—she shuddered just speaking the words—"and his mother's mind ruined by all of it."

Malcolm Ramsey raised his head very slowly. "Was he ever imprisoned?" he asked.

"Yes, he was. And there's an incredible story behind that. He was to be sent into exile in the Australian colonies. But my great-grandmother—her name was Morag Macpherson—she obtained his release."

Her listener shuddered and his eyes had grown fevered.

"I'm sorry," she stammered. "I ought not to have—"

He clamped his hands on her shoulders. "Did your grandmother release him? Bring the pardon herself?"

"Yes," Flora gulped, feeling wretched. "That's part of the story. They were loading the wagon to carry the men to the ships that would take them from Scotland forever. He was walking in the line and she ran up and stopped him, and pulled him away."

"Fort Augustus?"

"Yes, at Fort Augustus. How did you know?"

The tension within relaxed. His eyes were wide with wonder. "He would not have gone to Australia," he said. "Most of the men ended up being shipped to the American colonies. That is where his friend, Hugh Ramsey, was sent. Hugh Ramsey, who had marched with him, starved with him, fought with him, and who followed next in the line and watched his friend being snatched from the jaws of hell by the courage and love of a beautiful girl."

"What are you saying?" Flora's heart was racing. "How do *you* know these thing?"

"My grandfather was Hugh Ramsey. He was made a bondsman in Virginia. When he became a free man after twelve long years he settled in South Carolina. At thirty-six he married. At thirty-eight his wife bore him a son. He named the lad Malcolm, after his beloved friend left behind in the homeland."

Flora shook her head, barely able to credit his story. But through the tears her eyes shone.

"It was somehow a symbol to him, one he sorely needed; a link of blood and spirit which he considered to be most sacred. And his son, my father, gave me the name in his turn."

"A link between me and thee, between my blood and thine." She touched the broad, tear-stained face.

"Between your spirit and my spirit." He breathed a ragged sigh. "The restored gospel forged the last link," he reflected.

"And you returned, returned to serve others, and therefore found me."

They were silent for a moment, contemplating what they had learned, in harmony of spirit. Flora sighed. "Would I could help you, as you have so often and generously helped me."

"You have. You have reminded me of why I am here, and what it is that I seek."

"What is it you seek?" she asked, waiting for his response with deep interest.

"I seek to do the will of the Lord, to serve him and my brothers and sisters." He shrugged his broad shoulders, but it was a little-boy gesture, and it tugged at her heart. "It is he who watches over us. I believe for a time I forgot that. Louisa has been taken home; it is well with her. 'Tis I who must yet endure, hold on, and remember that my life is in the Lord's hands, and he will not fail me."

Nor me! Flora realized for the first time. *Nor any of his children who seek him.* She recalled with sudden clarity how, when she was a child, Morag used to tell her: "We can do what we must do, child, you and I."

She repeated the words to Malcolm Ramsey and he smiled, tears in his eyes. "Aye, my dear lass, that we can. But, as for myself, I need his help to do it."

Flora bent over and kissed his cheek. "So do I," she said. "I know that now."

She wondered, riding back in the dark carriage through the quiet streets, how it had been with her great-grandmother. Had she, too, felt the need for assistance when loss and suffering assailed her? Had heaven helped her, and had she felt and acknowledged that aid? Then, stepping out of the carriage into the cool air, with the moon painting patterns of gold across the shadowed pavement, she remembered: "I learned to pray at a young age." So Morag had often told her. *Oh, Grandmother,* her heart yearned, *you knew what I have been struggling to learn for myself. Despite faith, despite prayer, I wish I had you beside me right now.*

Trembling with loneliness and a sad, tender longing, Flora entered the house, feeling somehow altered—different from the woman she had been when she left brief, interminable hours ago.

22

She stayed all the next day and the following night with Colin, as well as the week's end, as she had planned. They were precious days, stolen from time, and she treasured them. He mended quickly; the concussion had not been serious and the wounds were not deep. But since he was invalided at home, they had much time together, albeit too many hours were occupied with the mysterious accident and the repercussions from it which they were already observing.

A man came forward the day following the accident, one of Colin's workers, who claimed to have seen John McCallum, one of Gavin Douglas's managers, in an Irish pub in intense conversation with one of Colin's night watchmen. Neither had seen nor recognized the worker. And another worker, a young married woman, told Ewen Fraser that her sister worked in Gavin's mill and, when he fired the Irishman, several of the workers heard him threaten to do harm to Colin Fraser, to get even with the whole Fraser clan.

Were the reports reliable? Were they sufficient enough evidence to take some sort of legal steps against Gavin? Ewen Fraser thought so, and he was anxious that some official action be taken, despite the complicating and tragic fact that the man accused was brother to the woman his son was to marry.

"All the more reason," he argued. "The man has indulged himself and let his angers and prejudices get quite out of hand. He must be stopped! And the earlier, the better. If he takes exception to your marriage, then what might he do?" He shook his head sadly, his long mustache waving. "You must not live in fear. 'Tis no way to begin a new life together."

Flora knew Mr. Fraser was right. Perhaps if the law—sane, ordinary, univolved people—were brought in, Gavin would come to his senses, realize he must let go, and allow them to live their own lives, as he expected to be allowed to live his.

Mr. Fraser insisted she go home in the carriage, with her horses tied behind. And the stubborn old coachman would not agree to come into the house for refreshment once they arrived.

"I know a fair tavern in the last village we passed through, and— no offense, miss—but I b'lieve I'd fare better there."

With a shake of her head she let him go. It felt good to be home again. Her heart was sore, and Ravenwood acted upon her like a tonic. The old house itself could renew her—the beauties, the memories, the very strength the house seemed to possess.

Nathan led the horses to the stables. Izzy came out to carry her bags in. "Where's Mother?" Flora asked.

"Upstairs with a headache."

"Doesn't she wish to come down and see me?"

Izzy glanced at her slantwise. "I'll go up and tell her you've arrived, miss."

"And my lad—where's Rory? Send him down to me quickly. I've missed him so much!"

She removed her coat, hat, and gloves and went into the small front sitting room, which was sunny even at this time of year. *What a lovely place Ravenwood is!* she thought proudly. *'Tis elegant, as Colin once said.* What was keeping them? She poked her head out into the hall, listening for footsteps. "Izzy? Rory? What is keeping you? Hurry down, please!"

The light child's patter never came. Izzy did not return. Nathan Forbes entered the room, and her mother, half-hidden behind his solid bulk, followed after. She did look ill, but something in her face made Flora's heart shrink.

"What is it?" She felt as if she were begging. "Is something wrong here?"

"You might say that, lass." Nathan's voice was gentle, but his eyes, usually dancing with warm lights, were empty and dull. "Rory is not here—at the house. Your brother has seen fit to remove him."

"What? What are you telling me, Nathan?" He could not be saying what she thought he was saying. That would be too monstrous, too unbearable.

"The lad is safe, but in another's keeping for the time being, I am told." Nathan's voice revealed nothing, and he would not meet her gaze.

"My brother has done this?"

"Yes, miss."

"On what authority?" Her voice sounded hoarse and her head was ringing. Nathan glanced at her mother.

Rowena's voice trembled and she twisted her handkerchief in her hands as she spoke. "Gavin came here and said you had allowed yourself to be baptized a Mormon, despite the kindness and sympathy he showed you at the time of Lilias's death, and that you are planning to marry a wicked man who is more deluded than you are."

Something turned to ice within Flora. "You know Colin, Mother. You know he is neither wicked nor deluded. You *like* Colin!"

Her mother fidgeted uncomfortably. "I don't know what to say, Flora. Gavin thinks you are not capable of caring for Rory in your present condition. 'This will bring her to her senses,' he said, 'and do her good in the end.' That's what he said."

"And you agree with him?"

Her mother looked miserable, but did not answer.

"You have no mind of your own, and certainly no feelings. You let him take Rory away!" It was a statement, a cry and an accusation, all at the same time.

"There is nothing I can do when Gavin sets his mind to something, Flora. You know that." Her voice held a child's impotent whine. Flora swayed and realized that Nathan's firm hands had steadied her.

"Where is my son?" she demanded. "Nathan, do you know anything about this?"

Neither would look at her, neither would answer.

"Where is my son?" Her voice had risen to a high pitch. There was a dizzy ringing inside her head. "He has no right! Gavin is a cruel, stupid man. I'm sure Rory is frightened and unhappy—and why should an innocent child suffer for anyone's sins, even mine?"

"Flora, please! It is no use at all to go on this way and upset yourself. Nothing at all can be done. Rory is fine, I am sure. We'll sort all this out with Gavin."

"You are sure? You are sure!" Flora paced the room, her mind reeling. "Get out of here, both of you! Get out of my sight!"

As soon as they disappeared she sank down to the floor and sobbed brokenly. *Please, Father,* she pleaded. *Not this, not now!* Without wanting to, she remembered Malcolm Ramsey's face when he said: "She called for me, and I was not there. She died without me." The horror ran with a thrill of pain through her system. The child had already suffered so much! Was Rory even now huddled somewhere, frightened, confused, crying for her? She felt she could bear her own pain. But the thought of his sent a terrible madness swirling inside her head.

Her own words came back like bitter bile to choke her. In the face of Elder Ramsey's pain she had been brave enough to say: "You and I can do what we must do!" But could she believe that now? Now, when the unbearable assailed her, and injustice shattered her defenses! She crawled to her knees, closed her eyes tightly, and attempted to pray. *At least help me to endure this,* she begged. *Comfort Rory, wherever he is, and keep him safe.*

She dreaded opening the door and facing whatever lay out there. She had no idea what to do or where to start. She had become suddenly a prisoner within the loved walls that had welcomed her. Tears filled her eyes again. It was late in the day and she was drained and tired, and not thinking well.

If she could somehow make it through the night she could return to Paisley tomorrow. Colin would know how to help her, and Colin's father. But meanwhile . . . meanwhile she must wait and suffer—while the child she loved was lost in a darkness she could not penetrate. And meanwhile someone right here, in this very house, was a traitor and an enemy. Was that enemy watching her now, prepared to report to Gavin her every move, her every reaction?

Nathan. Nathan, who was always there with her mother, who all at once would not meet her eyes, who had access to everything at Ravenwood, and authority to utilize that access. She placed her hand on her stomach, feeling suddenly sick inside.

At length, smothered by the confining boundaries of the room and her own stifling thoughts, Flora opened the door and moved with a cat's cushioned stealth down the hall, empty and silent. The whole house seemed silent around her. *Bereft.* That was the word which came to her. Bereft of the music of childhood laughter, bereft of love.

She went up to her room. To be certain, all in the household were keeping out of her way. She felt hungry, but would not go herself into the kitchens in search of food. She walked to her window. Night had begun to settle. A long gray veil, shaken out by some unseen hand, was creeping closer and closer, leaving only a band of dull white between it and the waiting land. If night's opiate, sleep, could rob her of this sorrow for even a few wayward hours, perhaps the release would renew her and bolster her strength to face a morning she dreaded.

As she dressed for bed she realized suddenly that morning might be too late. If Gavin had in place someone who was spying on her, would her attempt to leave in the morning be thwarted? That seemed a possibility she ought to consider. But what alternatives were left her? Dare she try to leave in the night?

The prospect of sneaking through the darkened house out into a yet darker night, attempting to saddle Rosie, skittish as she would be, without the aid of light, without provoking detection seemed ludicrous to her. And, if somehow accomplished, well, what then? Her experience coming home alone at night from the Mormon meeting was still strong enough in her memory to deter her from another lone venture, however worthy the cause.

At last she determined to slip out and leave just before first light. To escape undetected was really all she needed to accomplish, and that seemed the best plan she could think of. She pulled back the covers and climbed into her bed. It felt cold to her touch, and she could not seem to get warm. She slept poorly, tossing and turning, dreaming and waking. When at last she admitted defeat and crawled out of bed her head ached and she felt weak and exhausted from lack of sleep. She dreaded the thought of a journey, dreaded the inevitable encounters and struggles that lay ahead. The darkness intimidated her, and with a dragging reluctance she made the required preparations. "We can do what we must do, we can!" she muttered through clenched teeth.

The hall was empty—had she expected it to be otherwise?—and the stairway, a cavernous black hole she must descend into. She dressed warmly, but the dawn air seeped into her, damp and penetrating. Near the old stables the shadows were deep still, and she skirted them, wishing the sun would top the far ridges and melt the frost and the shadows.

She stepped inside, blinking against the dust and the dim, murky light. She heard the rustle of something moving behind her, but a firm, warm hand covered her mouth before she could cry out or even move. Nathan stood close to her, his eyes burning and wide-awake in his weathered face.

"Listen to me, Flora, quickly and carefully. I know where Gavin has the lad."

Her wide eyes questioned him.

"Paisley. The home of one of his foremen. Weren't you going there, anyway?" He removed his hand from her mouth. "I'm sorry, lass, but I knew you'd be frightened. 'Twas all I could do back at the house to watch you suffer and not tell you then."

She stood watching him, undecided.

He drew closer and lifted her chin so that her eyes looked into his.

"How do I know you are not Gavin's man, and leading me into a trap, taking me to him, taking me right where he wants me?"

"You don't know that, Flora. You can only make a decision and follow it. I've never been 'Gavin's man.' You've always been able to trust me." He held her gaze as he continued. "I've been doing my own investigation of the Mormon religion."

He answered her startled response. "Aye, I've attended meetings in some of the villages round here. I've read the Book of Mormon. I had made up my mind to step forward, but then your brother showed up that first time. I saw him plotting with a certain person in the household, and I thought I would hold back and see what they'd do."

"Is that when my clothes were stolen?"

"Aye, lass. When that happened I told myself, 'Nathan, you had best be patient and serve the mistress a while from this vantage point.'"

Flora was beginning to see. "Gavin trusted you, or at least did not suspect you. And the . . . other person, the . . . conspirator?" Flora shuddered.

"A sorry little thing, really. Young Judith who works in the kitchens and laundry."

The girl Flora had heard singing as she hung out the clothes!

"Gavin told her he would dismiss her if she did not cooperate with him, and double her wage if she did. The poor lass had no will to resist. Then he proceeded to flatter her. You know Gavin."

"Aye, only too well."

"I have the horses saddled and ready." Nathan glanced with concern at the high square of window; the sky had grown considerably lighter while they talked. "I dared not leave with you and assist you sooner, for fear Judith would continue in her office. So, I've made other plans." Nathan moved as he spoke, in that supple way of his, leading the animals forward, helping Flora to mount. "The constable in Kingussie is a friend of mine." He half turned, and for the first time in a long while Flora saw tiny pricks of light dance in his eyes. "Fact is, he's also investigating the Mormon religion. He it was who gave me a copy of the Book of Mormon a wee bit back."

So that had been the exchange Flora had seen and fretted over that day in the village!

"He'll be here soon after the sun's up, and take young Judith into custody. He knows enough of what's been going on to wring a confession from her, I believe. Are you ready?"

Flora nodded.

"Follow me closely. We'll go a roundabout way I know."

No one saw them leave Ravenwood. After a few yards the path through the woods hid them completely from view. Nathan knew where he was going, but still he had to pick his way carefully in the uncertain light. But this path was shorter than the usual route and narrowed the journey by nearly an hour. When they drew up before Colin's house the city was still stretching itself, rumbling and screeching and whistling into motion that would yet reach a humming, almost fevered pitch. As Nathan helped her dismount he wrapped his arms round her and pulled her close for a moment. "Poor lass, you're chilled to the bone," he murmured. "But never you fear. Things will work out. 'Tis clear to me—me, who's been watching—that someone up there is looking out for you, lass."

His words thoroughly warmed her. What was it Malcolm Ramsey had said? "The Lord will grant you your righteous desires."

With an optimism she had not felt before, she approached Colin's house.

23

The discussions were long, drawn out, and painful, but they all boiled down to one thing: Gavin had overstepped himself. He had offended the law, trampled on people's rights, caused injury, suffering, and damage. Let the law take care of him, as it rightfully should. Why, carrying off Rory even fell into the realm of kidnapping. Flora was the child's legal guardian. What Gavin did was highly illegal—what Gavin did, what Gavin did. It mattered not who said it: Colin, his father, Nathan, Elder Ramsey, Kenneth, the friendly and willing witnesses. There was no doubt in anyone's mind. Why should she alone have this feeling of sorrow and loss?

Colin, who had been watching her carefully, said, "He's your brother, Flora. You were raised together as children. The sorrow you feel is a natural thing."

Yet it surprised even herself. Because of the pain he had caused her she wanted to hate him. She had thought she wanted to see him suffer. She had not anticipated what she was feeling right now.

Rory, Nathan felt sure, was at the house of Gavin's most trusted foreman, and though Flora fought a restless longing to fly to him, she knew Gavin and the whole matter must be confronted head on, in its entirety, before she would be free to claim the abducted child.

Flora drew Colin close to her. "Could I speak with Gavin first, Colin? Perhaps just you and I."

"Absolutely not. What are you thinking of, Flora?"

"I'm thinking of him. I don't want him to hate me forever. If we send the authorities in right now I may never see him again—and that thought terrifies me. If I could explain . . ."

"He would not listen to you, lass," Nathan said gently.

"But I must at least try! Otherwise, for the rest of my life I'll regret it, I'll wonder if—"

Colin shook his head at her. The others waved her protest aside.

"Let her go."

Flora looked up. The voice that had spoken was one which had grown familiar and dear to her. "I believe Flora is right. We owe her that much." Malcolm Ramsey smiled at her out of his sad, gentle eyes. "Who knows? Perhaps we owe mercy that much as well."

It was arranged that Colin would accompany her to Carmichael and Son. Malcolm Ramsey and Nathan would wait round the corner in Ewen Fraser's carriage. But when they arrived at the mill Colin was informed that Gavin Douglas was not in, nor was he expected to be in all day. Fighting a sense of foreboding, Flora rode in silence while the three men in the carriage with her made small talk amongst themselves. She was praying silently as the carriage bore her along.

Gavin's home was a nice, impressive building, a gift from Agatha's parents when the young people were married, although Gavin had money inherited from Morag as well. The carriage pulled round the corner, out of sight. Flora stood on the unfamiliar porch clinging to Colin's hand.

"You are certain you want to be alone with him?" he asked one more time.

"Yes, I'm certain. You wait in the hall, and say a prayer for me."

A housekeeper came to the door and peered at them sharply. "What may I do for you?" she asked grudgingly.

"Tell Mr. Douglas his sister is here and wishes very much to see him," Flora replied, forcing a kind look in response to the woman's dour expression.

They waited long minutes until she returned and said simply, "He will receive you in the library, ma'am."

When she entered the room Gavin stood stiff and formal beside the fireplace mantel, leaning against it, really. He gave her a curt nod of his head.

"I have come to explain some things to you, Gavin. Things that are happening, that I think you should know of." She paused and swallowed nervously.

"Go on."

She told him of her terrible homecoming, her factor's discovery of Judith's treachery and the steps he had taken, her return here with Nathan Forbes—she told him everything, even of the charges that were being prepared against him for the things he had done. When she reached the part about the witnesses who could testify concerning his involvement in the factory accident, he turned his back on her with a brusque, angry movement and pounded his fist on the mantelpiece, but he uttered no word at all.

That made it more difficult, speaking to his back, but she pushed forward and spared nothing, making the legalities plain, drawing for him a clear picture of his guilt and peril. She had rehearsed it all in her mind. As she stumbled through she kept her voice even and gentle. She wanted time to slip in her feelings, express some kindness to him along with the weight of indictment and pain. At several points she expected him to turn and lash out at her with a tirade of hatred and hot words. But he remained stiff and motionless. Flora was becoming uncomfortable. She paused and drew a deep breath, and at last he spun round to face her.

She steeled herself, cowered inwardly before him. Then she heard his soft moan and watched his hard face crumple. He dropped to his knees at her feet.

"No more, Flora, not today. I cannot bear it! I am a heartbroken man. I have nothing to live for, my life is—"

"Gavin, what is it?" She put her hands on his shoulders and shook him, for the wild look in his eyes had sent a cold terror through her.

"Agatha is dying. She took sick with the cholera a week ago. It's rampant in the city—harbored in the filthy hovels of the laborers!"

She shuddered; his cold hatred mixed with anguish was a terrible sound.

"I have done everything for her, but she keeps failing, failing!" He pounded the floor with his fist. "This morning the doctor said he can do nothing for her, and 'tis only a matter of time."

And I come! Flora shivered. *The self-righteous, avenging angel.*

Gavin rested his head in her lap. She could feel his terrible trembling. "Flora, don't let her die! For mercy's sake. She is all I have, really. She's all I love."

Flora knew how true his words were. Holding her breath she said softly, "I can help her if you mean it, if you will allow me."

His voice was muffled against her skirt; he did not dare to look up. "Tell me what you speak of."

"The Mormon elders heal people." She felt his whole body stiffen. "It has been done many times in this city; you have heard of instances, Gavin. But I saw it done with my own eyes."

He stirred. She knew he was listening carefully. "I watched Malcolm Ramsey bring Rory back from the brink of death when there was no other hope."

He lifted his face, bleared and blotchy with tears. She thought he would rave and curse her. But his eyes were fevered. "Bring him at once," he said.

Then she knew for a certainty the one human thing left about him: his love for his wife. She pushed him aside gently and arose. "Do you mean it? You will allow them to do what they do, and treat them with courtesy?"

"Them?"

"Colin. He is out in the hall waiting for me. He will bring Elder Ramsey; it will only take a few minutes."

"You have my word," Gavin said, and she knew he meant it.

"Wait here," she told him, and slipped out of the room.

Although Colin's eyes grew wide with wonder, he hastened to do as she requested. In the space of a few breathless moments both men stood in her brother's library. Malcolm Ramsey held a copy of the Book of Mormon in his hands.

"I would like to have a few moments to pray and prepare ourselves," he said to Gavin. "Then we will go up to your wife." He could see the anguished curiosity in the man's eyes, but Gavin's pride prevented him from asking any questions. "You are welcome to remain in the room with us," Malcolm continued, his voice low and gentle. "We will anoint her head with a small portion of oil consecrated to the healing of the sick," he explained. "Then, placing our hands on her head, we will use our authority to invoke God's blessing. His power alone can heal her."

Gavin gave no sign of what he was thinking. "I will wait with her for you to come," he replied, then turned and left them.

Malcolm asked Colin to read a few passages from the volume of scripture he carried. Then the three knelt in prayer, and the whole while Elder Ramsey was speaking Flora prayed one thing only, over and over again: *Let my faith be enough. Let my faith suffice for his lack, and have mercy, Father, that this healing might serve thy purposes and work some kind of good.*

And so it happened. Flora stood and watched for the second time the hand of the Lord. She felt the light in the room, she felt the light within her. And Gavin's face reflected that light, and his joy embraced it for one perfect, sanctified moment.

Agatha opened her eyes and asked for him. They left the two together, but when the men were ready to go, Flora insisted on staying. She would wait in the library until her brother came down.

Malcolm Ramsey went back to the carriage; Colin sat on the hard settle in the hall—he would not desert her at this point. She waited a long time. She read passages from the Book of Mormon Elder Ramsey had left on the sofa; she prayed; she leaned back and closed her eyes and tried to rest. At last she heard the door handle turn, and Gavin walked into the room.

"She is resting now. I sent for the doctor. She will be all right."

Confirmation, Flora thought to herself. "I'm so glad." She smiled at Gavin, trying to touch him with her love. "I would like Nathan to go get Rory. Will you give me a note for your man, releasing Rory to Nathan and placing him back in my care?"

Her heart was pounding, but he offered no objection; rather, he sat at his desk, wrote on a paper, then folded it and handed it to her.

"I should thank you," he said. "I do thank you." The words came hard for him.

"I know you do, Gavin." Her voice was vibrant with tenderness. "I will be in the city for a few days. I would like to do anything I might to help. I would like to visit Agatha when she is stronger."

Gavin nodded slightly.

"Would that be all right?" she pressed.

"Yes, of course." He was wary, already wary.

"You know, it was not I. I did nothing, Gavin."

She picked up the Book of Mormon that had been lying on the couch beside her. "If I leave this book with you, will you read it?"

His features instantly contorted and he backed away from her. "I will not touch that book!"

"You cannot deny what you felt upstairs, Gavin. I saw it in your eyes, I saw it glowing—"

"That is no matter!" He waved her words away with a hard gesture. "What I felt, I felt. But I want no more of it."

"How can you say that?" Her childlike astonishment was clear in her voice.

"I can say it with ease," he responded. "I have my own life, Flora. I know well what I want, and your Mormon religion has no part in it."

She sat speechless. "If you left that book," he continued, "I would be afraid to read it, for feat I might believe what it said."

You know not what you say, you know not what you do! Her heart trembled.

"You go your way, Flora—yes, go your way. But let me still go mine."

Lean not unto thine own understanding. . . . Thy will, not mine, be done. . . . "What is it you seek?" she had asked Malcolm Ramsey. And his answer had been, "I seek to do the will of the Lord, to serve my brothers and sisters."

Her heart wept for this brother who stood before her. *You will never be happy,* she cried out to him silently. *Yes, Agatha has been restored to you. But what use will you make of the gift? What will you give, that you might know happiness and not only getting and taking?*

"Come, Flora." He held out his hand to her. She rose, the book tucked under her arm. *A truce,* his eyes said, staring purposefully into hers. *When I give my word, I keep it. I will distress you no more.* He would never have spoken the words aloud, but the understanding between them was clear.

"I still thank *you,* Flora," he said, as he walked to the door with her. "I always will."

Colin stood stiffly as they entered. Gavin leaned forward and shook his hand. "Invite me to the wedding when it happens, will you?"

Colin gave him a long look. "I will," he answered at last.

Suddenly Flora found herself outside the door, looking around her at the ordinary activities of an ordinary day. She felt weak and leaned against Colin for support. How strong he felt, how immovable. He was watching her closely, searching her face.

"You are still the loveliest woman I ever set eyes upon, Flora. Whatever happened in there, one thing I know—you and I have a grand future together." He shook his long black hair. "When I went to that Mormon meeting in Kingussie I had been praying for a long time. I wanted something more in my life. My parents are wonderfully matched; they've had an incredible marriage. And Kenneth and Janet have been so happy together." His eyes grew gentle and serious. "I was afraid—afraid life would cheat me, pass me by in some way. After all, could I expect Fraser luck to hold?" He smiled and took her arm and started walking.

"What exactly are you trying to tell me?"

"I guess I'm trying to tell you that Heavenly Father answered my prayers that night, Flora, as well as yours. I had been praying that I would be led to a choice, remarkable woman to marry, and that somehow I would know her."

Without closing her eyes she could see his face bending over her that night, his kind, wonderful eyes, the overpowering sense of his presence. *Help someone to find me,* she had prayed. *Someone good, someone I can trust.*

He steered her toward the waiting carriage. Malcolm Ramsey stuck his head out. "Haven't we someplace to go?"

Flora dug into her pocket for the paper Gavin had given her. "We certainly do," she said, smiling at all of them, weak with the love and the joy she felt. An ordinary day? How could she possibly have thought that? She glanced at the people around her: the young man crossing the street, the quiet woman pushing a baby carriage before her, the two scruffy boys playing marbles in a circle of dust at the busy street's edge. Each was distinct, and alive, and precious. And so was she. Today was her life. Not the past, not the unseen tomorrows. This breathless, beating moment, and no more. But it was enough. She would take it with gladness.

Colin tugged at her hand. "Come with us, Flora!" He smiled. "Goodness, your face is shining!"

He planted a kiss on her cheek as he handed her into the carriage, then sat down and moved close beside her—part of her, one with her, as he always would be.